Keyword Spotting System in Speech Mining

Dr.K.A. Senthil Devi,

Assistant Professor, Department of Computer Science,

Gobi Arts & Science College,

Gobichettipalayam.

Dr.B. Srinivasan,

Associate Professor, Department of Computer Science,

Gobi Arts & Science College,

Gobichettipalayam.

Published by

Keyword Spotting System in Speech Mining

ISBN 978-93-86638-74-8

Authors

Dr.K.A. Senthil Devi

Dr.B. Srinivasan

Bonfring

309, 2nd Floor, 5th Street Extension, Gandhipuram,

Coimbatore-641 012.

Tamilnadu, India.

E-mail: info@bonfring.org

Website: www.bonfring.org

Phone: 0422 4213231

Preface

This book brings all of the elements of keyword spotting in speech mining together in a single volume. It brings together the fields of speech and data mining which are needed for spoken keyword spotting.

This book is written for general readers, students who want to learn about new technologies in keyword spotting to provide intelligent access to obtain potential knowledge in large speech collection. Keyword spotting is the field of speech mining used in many areas including defense, commerce, command controlled devices, audio document indexing and searching, information retrieval, telephone routing, monitoring broadcast news, verifying credit card transaction, routing multimedia files, music information retrieval, human-computer interaction, quality control, automatic operator services, real time keyword monitoring, and soon.

We shall gratefully acknowledge any suggestions to further increase the utility of the book. This book will provide satisfactory and meaningful reading to the students and will be of immense help to them and others related to the field.

Acknowledgement

We thank the Management and Principal of Gobi Arts and Science College for providing me the moral support and encouragement.

We also express our heartiest thanks to our family members for their help and co-operation to complete this work successfully.

Finally, I am grateful to my publisher, Bonfring Publications for taking keen interest in the publication of the book in such an excellent form and so expeditiously.

Authors Profile

Dr.K.A. Senthildevi holds Ph.D in Speech Data Mining and was received her post graduate M.C.A., and under graduate Bsc(Phy) degrees from Bharathiar University, Coimbatore, India. She is qualified NET and SET in the field of Computer Science. She has 20 years of academic experience and currently working as Assistant Professor at Gobi Arts and Science College, Gobichettipalayam, India. She is the Author of "Computer Networks", book focusing on students in Networks. She has more than 15 research publication to her credit in international journals and conferences.

Dr.B. Srinivasan did his M.C.A., in Gobi Arts & Science College, Gobichettipalayam and Ph.D., in Computer Science at Vinayaka Missions University, Salem. He is working as an Associate Professor in Computer Science, Gobi Arts & Science College, Gobichettipalayam. He has 26 years of experience in teaching and 19 years in research experience. He has published 70 research papers in national and international journals. He has guided 65 M.Phils and 7 Ph.Ds. His area of interest includes Network Security and Automata Theory.

<table>
<tr><th>Chapter</th><th>Contents</th><th>Page No</th></tr>
</table>

CHAPTER 1

INTRODUCTION

1.1. Introduction to Speech Mining

Speech has become one of the most important human communication media. Due to advancements in recent technology, very large quantities of speech can be collected and stored digitally. This large volume of speech cannot be efficiently reviewed by human beings. New technologies are required to provide intelligent access for obtaining potential knowledge from the large speech storage.

Data mining techniques are concerned with discovering patterns and extracting useful information automatically from data. Data mining is involved in the areas of statistics, artificial intelligence, and machine learning. The mining research has started to penetrate new grounds in areas of speech and audio processing, as well as spoken language dialog.It has gained interest due to the availability of plenty of audio data. The existence of such large amounts of speech data has created a need for efficient and accurate data mining tools for extracting useful information, knowledge and keywords from the data. The typical need for mining is to search or browse through the speech data, locating specified topics, words, phrases, or identifying speakers. The technology is now highly attractive for a variety of speech mining applications.

Keyword spotting (KWS) is the identification of predefined keywords in spoken utterances. Spoken keyword spotting is a technologically relevant problem in speech data mining which is essential to identify the occurrences of specified keywords excellently from lots of hours of speech contents such as meetings, lectures, etc.[Jansen, A and Niyogi, P, 2009]. KWS generally carries some kind of classification based upon speech features which are usually obtained via time-frequency representations. The system can be used equally and efficiently on any language as it does not depend on an underlying language model or grammatical constraints.

Challenges in KWS field are complicated because human conversation contains not only irrelevant words, but also non-intentional sounds like cough, exclamations and noise. If only the embedded information can be extracted by some means, computation can be much more efficient and robust. However people's speech is not in terms of isolated words. They speak continuously and there are no distinct word boundaries in speech which make identification more difficult. Unlike keyword spotting in written document, speech keyword spotting systems tend to be much more difficult because of the large variation of pronunciations, even from the same speaker, depending on the context and mood of the speaker. The research on keyword spotting is carried out to overcome these kinds of challenges.

Keyword spotting systems can be divided into two main categories: speaker dependent and speaker independent. Speaker dependent keyword spotting models are developed for a specific speaker and hence are not meant to apply for other speakers. Speaker independent keyword spotting models need to be more generic and hence need more complex design. Some examples of these kinds of systems can be voice dialing, voice command systems, audio search engines, etc. Keyword spotting also has many direct applications such as audio document retrieval, telephone routing, speech indexing and information retrieval.

The proposed research is carried out to address the issues like retrieving time, extracting time-frequency based information from non-stationary speech signals and reducing the long computational time taken by the keyword spotting system. The research work proposes different speaker independent acoustic keyword spotting models using wavelet packet decomposition, multi-wavelet packet entropies with sliding window model and Neural Network classifiers. These models are different from the Hidden Markov Model (HMM) and template matching based systems which are widely used in keyword spotting system design. As a result, the proposal of keyword spotting system with multi wavelet packet entropies and neural network is proved to be a novel method.

1.2.   Overview of Audio Mining

Audio mining is a growing technology, due to the voluminous increase in the amount of audio content on the internet and other sources. Audio mining is a technique by which the content of an audio signal can be automatically analyzed and searched. Audio mining research includes speech processing and language processing algorithms with data mining techniques. It helps in the areas of prediction, search, explanation, learning and language understanding. The growth in audio mining has led to algorithmic advances in automatic speech recognition have also been a major, enabling technology.

Audio mining is a speaker independent, speech recognition technique that is used to search or recognize audio or video [Manpreet K M et al, 2013]. Audio mining systems can be created to infer knowledge automatically from audio data, analyze, report application performance, adapt and improve over time with minimal or zero human involvement. It is most commonly used in the field of automatic speech recognition, where the analysis tries to locate any speech in word or phrase within the audio. Fundamental research in areas of clustering, prediction, classification, summarization, knowledge retrieval, pattern discovery, learning and language understanding of audio become important in business processes. A variety of multimedia sources like Web casts, conversations, music, meeting, voice messages, lectures, television and radio that facilitates the access of audio data can further ignite research ideas. Effective techniques for mining speech, audio, and dialog data have impact on numerous business and government applications. The technology for monitoring conversational audio to discover patterns, capture useful trends and generate alarms is essential for intelligence and law enforcement organizations as well as for enhancing call center operations. It is useful for a digital object that identifies, analyzes, monitors, and tracks customer preferences and interactions to establish better customized sales and technical support strategies. It is also an essential tool in media content management to search large volumes of audio files to find information, keywords, and news.

Audio can be in the form of radio, speech, music, etc. Audio of common birds and pet animals have been recorded casually in audio files. Due to the continuous, dynamic and non-structured nature of audio, audio files must be represented with spectral coefficients to process further with data mining techniques. There are variant features to represent characteristics of speech in numeric forms. The audio mining system runs at a speed that is several times higher than that of traditional system. Hence, large quantities of audio or speech can be searched for in a short time.

1.2.1. Classifications of Audio Mining

Audio mining can be classified into various types as shown in figure 1.1

Figure 1.1: Classifications of Audio Mining

Speech Mining

Mining on speech is a research field that aims to bridge the gap between the speech processing methods and text data mining methods. In this era of internet, the speech data that grows rapidly demands new technologies and algorithms to access and extract meaningful information from the huge data. Speech mining is the process of searching and analyzing the contents of the voluminous, large speech data to identify patterns and associations, retrieve keywords and useful information [Dai Sheng Hui et al, 2011]. The existence of such large amount of speech data has created a need for efficient and accurate data mining tools to extract useful information, knowledge and keywords from the data. The typical mining process is required to search or browse through the data, locate specified topics or to identify the speakers.

Mining of multi speaker data collected from broadcasts, recorded lectures, meetings and telephone conversations are essential areas of research. Mining heterogeneous spoken data for the purpose of extracting business information is a fertile growth area for new research initiatives at many research and industrial labs around the world.

Keyword spotting is an excellent technology in speech data mining. Keyword spotting is well a suited technology to process large amount of speech such as real time monitoring audio document indexing in data mining [Halima Bahi et al, 2009]. KWS is used to locate occurrences of keyword in speech signal [Shao ed al, 2007]. Though it is similar to speech recognition, the additional signal information around the words of interest are ignored [Ramachandran and Mammone, 1995].

Voice Data Mining

Voice data mining is a multi-lingual voice processing system that is efficient in mining specific keywords amidst a huge audio repository. It deals with the need to organize, search and retrieve collection of spoken documents such as recorded lectures and telephonic conversations, TV or radio archives in an effective and efficient manner [Ajay Divakaran and Koji Miyahara, 2004]. The voice mining technology will be very useful when handled with highly secured audio information and documents in major enterprises. By recognizing critical speech portions, it assists human operators in real time voice to improve operational efficiency by reducing the time, cost and effort. Generally, it automatically extracts portions of a speech or conversation that are of interest or importance.

Music Mining

The research on music information retrieval has gradually evolved to address the challenges of effectively accessing and interacting large collections of music and associated data, such as styles, artists, lyrics, and reviews. Musical audio mining is related to the identification of perceptually important characteristics of a piece of music such as melodic, harmonious or rhythmic structure [Tao Li and Lei Li, 2010]. Searches can then be carried out to find pieces of music that are similar in terms of their melodic, harmonic and/or rhythmic characteristics.

Music data mining presents a variety of approaches to successfully employ data mining techniques for the purpose of music processing. The multifaceted nature of music information often need algorithms and systems using sophisticated signal processing and data mining techniques to extract more useful information.

Video Mining

Video data contains several kinds of data such as video, audio and text. Video mining is used for the unsupervised discovery of patterns in audio-visual content. The motivation for such discovery comes from the success of data mining techniques in discovering hidden patterns [Daria Hemmerling et al, 2016]. Furthermore, surveillance video often consists of events that are not known beforehand and is hence an obvious target for unsupervised discovery of patterns, which, in this case, are events. With video mining we would hope to discover the interesting events in the video without a priori knowledge of what those events are.

Conversation Mining

Conversation mining can be defined as the analysis of conversations in a conference or in a call center. The conversations in a call center are analyzed to understand various issues discussed the intent of the caller, resolution of the issues and etc. To address the problems, speech recognition, Natural Language Understanding (NLU), data mining, machine learning, topic modeling and other techniques are used. With conversation mining, it is possible, by extracting data from these conversations, to automate and process this data in real-time and at scale.

1.2.2. Demand for Audio Mining

With the voluminous increase in the amount of audio data, there is a need to explore new methods for accessing and mining these data. Audio mining refers to the processing of large amounts of speech resulting in useful information for humans. Recently, a number of researches have been developed in audio mining to reduce manual accessing time and effort. The demand for audio mining systems comes from a range of areas spanning the public and private sectors, defense, commerce, social and recreational domains. The benefits of such systems are dramatic and wide reaching in each of these fields.

A major demand for audio mining systems is in the analysis of telephone conversations recorded by customer call centers. As these centers collect huge amounts of data regularly, the only possible way to analyze the content or nature of a significant proportion of the calls is with an automated system. Other commercial applications include automatic processing of telephone surveys and monitoring of broadcast news or radio. The Internet is another medium set to benefit from audio mining technology.

1.3.   Basic Components of Audio Mining

Data mining techniques on audio, speech, music and video data are generally used to achieve two kinds of tasks[Pradnya P. Sondwal, 2015] namely Descriptive Mining and Predictive Mining.

Descriptive Mining characterizes the general properties of the data in the database. Descriptive model mostly identifiespatterns or relationships in datasets. It serves to explore easily the properties of the data examine dearlier.

Predictive Mining serves to infer to the current data in order to infer predictions. The prediction output can be of numeric value or in a categorized form. The predictive model is the supervised learning functions which predict the targetvalue.

Both modalities have some basic components as shown in figure 1.2 to perform mining on various audio data types. These components are discussed below.

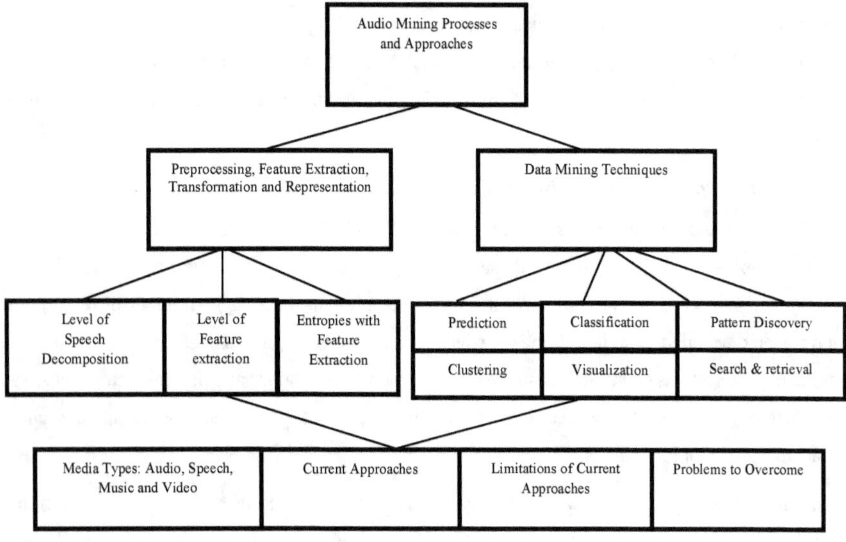

Figure 1.2: Basic Components of Audio Mining

1.3.1.   Preprocessing

Data preprocessing is a data mining technique that transforms raw data into an understandable format. Real-world data is often incomplete, inconsistent, and/or lacking in certain behaviors or trends, and is likely to contain many errors. Data preprocessing is a proven method of resolving such issues.

Tasks in Data Preprocessing

- **Data cleaning**: Data is cleansed through processes such as filling in missing values, smoothing the noisy data, identifying or removing outliers or resolving the inconsistencies in the data.
- **Data integration**: Different data are put together and the conflicts within them are resolved using multiple databases, data cubes, or files.
- **Data transformation**: Data is normalized, aggregated and generalized.
- **Data reduction**: The volume of data is reduced but the same or similar analytical results are produced.
- **Data discretization**: A part of data is reduced and the numerical attributes are replaced by nominal ones.

1.3.2. Transformation

Data transformation is the process of converting data or information in one format into another. Signal speech data transformation is used to convert a time domain function to a frequency domain functions and vice versa. A signal can be converted from time domain into frequency domain using mathematical operators called transforms. Transformations are applied to signals to obtain further information from that signal thatis not readily available in the raw signal. The most common transformation used in the frequency domain is the Fourier transformation.

Fourier transformation is used to convert a signal of any shape into a sum of infinite number of sinusoidal waves. Since analyzing sinusoidal functions is easier than analyzing general shaped functions, this method is widely used tool for analyzing the components of a stationary signal. But it cannot be used for the analysis of non-stationary signals. The wavelet transform is the most recent solution to overcome the shortcomings of the Fourier transform. In this research work, the wavelet transformation plays an important role in the design of keyword spotting algorithms.

1.3.3. Feature Extraction

Speech signals are quasi-stationary signals. When speech signals are examined over a short period of time, their characteristics are stationary; but, when examined over a longer period of time the characteristics changes. They reflect the different speech sounds being uttered. Features are extracted from the speech signals on the basis of short term amplitude spectrum. These features carry the characteristics of the useful information regarding speech. Feature extraction is the most important phase in speech processing system.

Features of speech are categorized into two types as features of time-domain speech signal and features of frequency-domain speech signal. [Poornima S, 2016]. Features of the Time-domain speech signal are short-time energy, short time zero crossing rate, short time auto correlation. Features of frequency domain are spectral centroid and spectral flux. These features can be extracted by using several methods such as Linear Predictive Codes (LPC), Perceptual Linear Prediction (PLP), Mel Frequency Cepstral Coefficients (MFCC), PLP-RASTA (PLP-Relative Spectra) etc. In the extraction of features, some parameters like PLP and MFCC consider the nature of speech while the others like LPC predict the future features based on previous features.

1.3.4. Data Mining Tasks on Audio

The tasks of Audio data mining can be classified into some broad groups. The task groups are as follows:

- Prediction
- Classification
- Clustering
- Search & retrieval
- Pattern discovery

Predication

Predictive analytics is an area of data mining that deals with extractions of information from data and using them to predict trends and behavior patterns. Often the unknown event of interest is in the future, but predictive analytics can be applied to any unknown event of interest whether it is of the past, present or future. Prediction encompasses a variety of statistical techniques from predictive modeling, machine learning,and data mining that analyze current and historical facts to make predictions about future or otherwise unknown events.

Classification

Classification classifies data to predefined classes. The classification application builds a model from the trained classes and uses that model to classify new objects into one of the predefined classes automatically. It is one of the most widely used data mining methods. The main focus of data mining techniques is on classification performance with large amount of data. Time series matching and classification have received much attention in speech processing activity. Spoken keyword spotting is one of the sequence classification applications. The classification task is performed in keyword spotting for classifying keywords from non-keyword contents of speech using similarity distance, neural network and other data mining techniques [Srivatsn Laxman and Sastry, 2006].Various audio features like Mel frequency Cepstral Coefficient (MFCC), Linear Predictive Coefficient (LPC), Spectral Flux, Band Periodicity, Zero Crossing Rate (ZCR) and etc., are used to classify speech data into various classes.

Clustering

Clustering is one of the most useful methods in the data mining process for discovering groups and identifying interesting distributions and patterns in the underlying data. It provides an attractive mechanism to automatically find some structure in large data sets that would be otherwise difficult to summarize. The main concern in the clustering process is to reveal the organization of patterns into sensible groups, which allow one to discover similarities and differences, as well as to derive useful inferences about them. In speech applications, a data mining system with clustering algorithm is used to derive useful patterns from speech database.

Search and Retrieval

Searching for sequences in large databases is an important task in data mining. Sequence search and retrieval techniques play an important role in interactive explorations. In content-based retrieval, the task is to search a large database of sequential data and retrieve from it sequences or subsequences similar to the given query sequence. In speech or audio applications, the individual elements of the sequences may be feature vectors of real numbers. When the sequential elements are feature vectors, Euclidean distance may be used for measuring similarity between two elements. In speech or audio signals, similar wounding patterns may produce feature vectors that have large Euclidean distances and vice versa. An elaborate treatment of distortion measure for Speech and Audio signals can be found. In speech applications, Dynamic Time Warping (DTW) is a systematic and efficient method that identifies which correspondence among feature vectors of two sequences is better when scoring the similarity between them.

Periodicity Detection

Periodicity detection has been a much researched problem in signal processing for many years. For example, there are many applications that require the detection and tracking of the principal harmony in speech and other audio signals. Standard Fourier and autocorrelation analysis-based methods form the basis of the most periodicity detection techniques that are currently in use in signal processing.

Pattern Discovery

Pattern Discovery is a pioneer in data mining and predictive analytics. Unlike in search and retrieval applications, in pattern discovery there is no specific query in hand with which to search the database. However, one concept that is found very useful in data mining is that of frequent patterns. Data mining is concerned with formulating useful pattern structures and developing efficient algorithms for discovering all patterns which occur frequently in the data. In some applications, acoustic pattern discovery methods are used for automatically discovering words from speech using a combination of graph clustering and base form searching.

1.3.5. Audio Data Sources

The audio consists of speech, music and various special sounds. Audio of common birds and pet animals have also been recorded casually in audio files. The audio data can have different formats like encoding types, compression types, numbers of channels, sampling rates, sample sizes, and playing times (duration) depending upon how the audio data was digitally recorded. Some of the audio resources are:

- Internet music stores that provide music samplings of CD quality
- Digital sound repositories
- Dictation and telephone conversation repositories
- Audio archives and collections (for example, for musicians)
- Digital video repositories
- Newscasts and sporting events
- Customer Interaction in call centers
- Recording of meetings
- Webcasts

1.3.6. Issues in Audio Mining

Audio mining process searches data many times faster than a human.However, its accuracy levels are relatively low, when used in real-time environment and some products are very expensive. Audio mining error rates vary widely depending onfactors such as background noise and cross talk.

Audio mining has problem in distinguishing the speakers, and time stamps are also not always accurate. Audio mining is domain specific, i.e., it is trained for specific applications or categories of speakers. These issues make audio mining task difficult.

1.4. Speech Data Mining Approaches

Speech data mining is defined as the nontrivial extraction of hidden and useful information from masses of speech data. Speechdata mining approaches can be roughly classified into three techniques, namely Keyword Spotting, Wake-Up-Word and Spoken Term Detection.

Keyword Spotting

In recent communication technologies, there is a need to spot a particular spoken word called as a keyword in the spoken utterance. The system designed for this particular task is called as Key Word Spotting (KWS) system. This is a specific application of Automatic Speech Recognition (ASR) [John Sahaya Rani Alex et al,2014]. Basically keyword spotting referred toas a problem of searching of keyword template in an unknown speech signal. This task of searching is very important and some of the application which does not require knowledge of whole contents of the unknown speech signal. In such cases, KWS system is used.

KWS is a technology used for locating occurrences of keyword in speech signal [Shao, J. et al 2007]. Keyword spotting plays an important role in audio indexing, Interactive Voice Response (IVR), call monitoring for national security system and other speech data mining applications [Jansen, A and Niyogi, P, 2009]. This problem issimilar to speech recognition, although ignoring the additional signal information around the words of interest.

The task of KWS is to search for various query words or terms in a large collection of heterogeneous audio archives rapidly and accurately. Many KWS approaches use word, syllable or phone level information. The word level spotting always requires additional training for unseen word [Szoke et al, 2005]. The phoneme provides ability to define new keyword easy, but such segment automatic boundary detection and classification in speech is not trivial [Greibus, M. et al, 2012]. Thesyllable is trade-off as it is easier to add.

Wake-Up-Word

Wake-Up-Word (WUW) uses speech commands to activate or wake up other systems by an alerting signal.The WUW speech recognition task is similar to keyword spotting. However, WUW is different in one important aspect of being able to discriminate the specific word/phrase used only in alerting context. Recently Wake-up-word (WUW) spotting for mobile devices has attracted much attention [V.Kepusk and T.Klein, 2009]. The aim is to detect the occurrence of very few or only one personalized keyword in acontinuous potential noisy audio signal. Wake-Up-Word (WUW) [V.Këpuska, 2006] bridges the gap between natural-language and other voice recognition tasks [V.Kepuska and T.Klein, 2008].

Spoken Term Detection

Spoken Term Detection (STD), defined by NIST as an audio mining technique, is employed for content based indexing. STD is aimed at open-vocabulary search over large collections of spoken documents. Similar to keyword spotting, STD finds a sequence of multiple words in the speech utterance [NIST, 2006].

The STD task is formulated as a detection task, requiring each occurrence to be specified by its start and endtimes. In addition, systems need to provide a score for each occurrence. Theinput for the task consists of raw audio files segments and alist of search terms. The systems are required to beimplemented in two phases: indexing and searching. The audio data is processed once during the indexing phase, without knowledge of the terms. The output index is stored and accessed during the searching phase, in order to retrieve the terms. The searching phase may be repeated multiple times for different terms so the efficiency of its implementation is very important.

1.5.   Speech Processing Technologies

1.5.1.   *Speech Data Processing*

Voice Activity Detection

Voice Activity Detection (VAD), also known as speech activity detection is a technique in speech processing in which the presence or absence of human speech is detected. Speech/non-speech detection is an unsolved problem in speech processing and affects numerous applications including robust speech recognition. VAD is widely used for achieving high speech coding efficiency and low-bit rate transmission in speech communication. The concepts of silence detection and comfort noise generation lead to dual-mode speech coding techniques. VAD is an important technology that enables variety of speech-based applications.

Word Boundary Detection

Word boundary detection is used to automatically identify the words and remove thesilence at the beginning and the end of the input signal. Accurate word boundary detection improves the accuracy of the speech recognition system and reduces the amount of processing. The main techniques used in word boundary detection are:

- Short time energy.
- Short time zero crossing rate.
- Short time pitches frequency.
- The combination of energy and the zero crossing rate thresholds.

Front-End Analysis

Front-End Analysis which known as Feature extraction is the first step in an automatic speech processing. It aims to extract features from the speech waveform that are compact and efficient to represent the speech signal. Since speech is a non-stationary signal, the feature parameters should be estimated over short-term intervals from 10ms to 30ms,in which speech is considered to be stationary. The major types of front-end processing techniques are:

- Linear Predictive Coding (LPC)
- Mel-Frequency cepstral coefficients (MFCC)
- Perceptual Linear Prediction (PLP)
- Energy and Zero Crossing Rate

Denoising Speech Signals

Delay-coordinates embedding of sets of coefficients of the measured signal are used as a data mining tool to separate structures that are likely to be generated by signals belonging to some predetermined data set. The embedding estimator in a windowed Fourier frame is designed and applied to speech signals heavily corrupted by white noise. The estimator performs well for a variety of white noise processes and noise intensity levels.

Speech Compression

Speech compression involves the compression of audio data in the form of speech. Speech is a somewhat unique form of audio data, with a number of needs which must be addressed during compression to ensure that it will be intelligible and reasonably pleasant to listen to. Speech compression is required in high-quality speech storage, long-distance communication, and message encryption.

Dimensionality Reduction

Real-world data, such as speech signals and images usually have a high dimensionality. In order to handle such real-world data adequately, its dimensionality needs to be reduced. Dimensionality reduction is the transformation of high-dimensional data into a meaningful representation of reduced dimensionality. Ideally, the reduced representation should have a dimensionality that corresponds to the intrinsic dimensionality of the data. The intrinsic dimensionality of data is the minimum number of parameters needed to account for the observed properties of the data. Dimensionality reduction is important in many domains, since it mitigates the curse of dimensionality and otherundesired properties of high-dimensional space

Speech Segmentation

Speech segmentation is the process of identifying the boundaries between words, syllables, or phonemes in natural spoken languages. The term applies both to the mental processes used by humans, and artificial processes of natural language processing. Speech segmentation is an essential preprocessing step in several speech processing applications with a significant impact. The quality of the segmentation affects the speech processing performance in several ways.

Diarization

Speaker diarisation (or diarization) is the process of partitioning an input audio stream into homogeneous segments according to the speaker identity. It can enhance the readability of an automatic speech transcription by structuring the audio stream into speaker turns and, when used together with speaker recognition systems, by providing the speaker's true identity. Speaker diarisation is a combination of speaker segmentation and speaker clustering.

Voice of Customer Analytics

Voice of Customer Analytics (VoCA) is developed to provide service in the area of CRM analytics. It provides unique capability to discover actionable business insights across various data sources ranging from calls to unstructured data to structured data. It encompasses advanced data mining algorithms such as data linking, text clustering, text annotation, sentiment mining and predictive modeling, that allows analysts to come up with actionable insights regarding customer churn, first call resolution, and key customer satisfaction or dissatisfaction drivers. It is used to analyze a variety of heterogeneous data sources such as, agent logs, call records, CSAT survey verbatim, other enterprise logs, CRM records and so on.

1.5.2. Research Areas in Speech Data Mining

Speech datamining research today involves in wide spread areas which require human machine interface. Applications like automatic call processing in telephone networks, and query based information systems that provide updated travel information, stock price quotations, weather reports, data entry, voice dictation, access to information: travel, banking, commands, automobile portal, speech transcription, blind people supermarket, railway reservations obtain fruitful outputs using speech mining in technologies. Research of data mining with Speech has involves the following areas:

- Speech Quality Measurement
- Error detection in dictation speech recognition
- Personalizing therapy of speech disorders

- Voice document retrieval and indexing
- Multimedia and telephony applications
- Telephony conversions in English automatically
- Searching large audio/media archives
- Language identification
- Gender recognition
- Speaker identification
- Speech emotion recognition

1.6. Keyword Spotting in Speech Data Mining

Spoken keyword spotting is a very crucial and promising branch in speech data mining and it is useful to retrieve the speech files which enclose the words associated with an application-specific domain. Keyword spotting requires significantly less processing power than transcription, and can therefore run at considerably faster speeds. It is essential to classify excellently lots of hours of speech contents such as meetings, lectures, etc.

The task of keyword spotting is to search for various query words or terms in a large collection of heterogeneous audio archives rapidly and accurately. KWS thus provides a satisfactory audio mining solution for spoken document retrieval tasks. Therefore, it is widely used in the on-line applications like real-time stream monitoring, as well as offline tasks like data the security services, telecommunication companies, radio stations, call-centers, broadcasting companies and other organizations. The input for these keywords may either be a text or an audio sample containing the keyword in isolation. Systems that use the latter kind of input are specifically termed spoken keyword spotting, or spoken query detection or query by example (QbE). KWS is classified according to the type of input speech content and t

The method used for spotting. A number of approaches like DTW, HMM, Neural Network, Vector quantization have been used in keyword spotting.

1.6.1. Types of Keyword Spotting

Keyword spotting system is broadly classified as:

- Speaker Dependent System
- Speaker Independent System

In Speaker Dependent System, the utterance and keyword are from the same speaker. In Speaker Independent system, the utterance and keyword are from the different speakers.

Based on the input speech data, KWS is also classified as:

- Keyword spotting in continuous speech
- Keyword spotting in isolated speech

In keyword spotting in continuous speech, the input spoken utterance and keywords may not be separated from other words and keyword spotting in isolated speech is applied when keywords can be separated from other words. KWS is also classified as:

- Unsupervised Keyword Spotting
- Supervised Keyword Spotting

Unsupervised keyword spotting identifies the keyword in the same group that are more similar to each other than those in other groups. Supervised keyword spotting technique is appropriate by having a specific target value to predict. The input for these systems may either be a text or a spoken utterance.

1.6.2. *Speech Recognition Versus Keyword Spotting*

Speech technology is used to recognize phonemes are words that are spoken in an audio file. An Automatic Speech Recognition (ASR) system is first trained with the entire content of audio file and audio mining searches are then carried out to locate specific words and phrases within the audio. Keyword spotting is concerned only with matched words and their counts. There is no need to transcribe the entire audio file. Continuous speech recognition requires complete decoding of speech signal and its output is a completely decoded sentence. Keyword spotting requires only to spot whether a keyword is present in a signal or not.

This difference separates keyword spotting from continuous speech recognition. Keywords are embedded in extraneous speech and may begin and end at any instant in the utterance making keyword spotting a non-trivial task. The keyword spotting in spoken data analyzes a given content and searches every speech segment in which one of pre-defined keywords is uttered. In general, the keyword spotting system provides more reliable performance than that of the continuous speech recognition system, while reducing computational time and intensity.

1.6.3. *Applications of Keyword Spotting*

Keyword Monitoring Applications

Keyword Monitoring Applications are required to continuously monitor real time audio to find the occurrences of a query keyword. The applications like telephone tapping, listening device monitoring and broadcast monitoring poseconsiderable challenges to KWS because in all these applications, noisy nature of the speech is being monitored. Telephone tapping and listening device monitoring applications are used by security organizations to detect criminal and malicious activities.

Broadcast monitoring is actively performed by commercial broadcast monitoring companies like cable television and commercial radio to locate some events that may be of interest to a client. KWS provides an excellent solution to all these keyword monitoring applications.

Call Center Management

Call center management requires a speech data mining system to generate a rich transcription utility function. One of the systems is speech differentiation module which differentiates the speech of interacting speakers. Another is a speech recognition module improving automatic recognition of speech of a speaker based on interaction with another speaker employed as a reference speaker. A transcript generation module generates a rich transcript based on recognized speech of the speakers. Mined speech data includes a number of interaction turns, customer frustration phrases, operator polity, interruptions, and contexts extracted from speech recognition results, such as topics, complaints, solutions, and resolutions. Mined speech data is useful in call center and product or service quality management.

Spoken Document Retrieval

Information can be extracted from large databases of audio messages by using speech data mining strategy. High Word-Error-Rate transcripts are often obtained on speech documents containing bad audio conditions. Call centers recordings contain a large variety of speakers with survey corpora contain a large variety of bad audio quality due to cell phones and surrounding noises, unconstrained speech, variable utterance length and numerous disfluences like hesitations, repetitions and corrections. Extraction of business intelligence from call center recording or extraction of opinion from telephone surveys are very difficult tasks on such corpora. The potential applications of speech mining in this context are important.

The system can work on very noisy automatic transcriptions of spoken messages. There is a need to quantify the extent of similarity between any two sequences. An application was developed to extract the distribution of user's opinions from telephone surveys. The system works on very noisy automatic transcriptions of spoken messages. Another application was developed for the removal of continuous noise from old music records. The data mining process allows one to discern between signal and noise portions of the audio material, so that the masking threshold level can be determined for each data frame allowing one to make the noise inaudible.

Audio Document Indexing

Audio document indexing is the task of rapidly searching an audio document database for keywords and topics of interest. This functionality is analogous to traditional text document indexing systems such as Google Internet search engine, but operates on audio documents instead. The need for efficient and fast audio document indexing is paramount in a world where audio and multimedia documents play a greater role in everyday life.

Command Controlled Devices

Command controlled devices monitor the ambient audio and react when they detect specific command words. Examples of command controlled devices are speech–enabled mobile phones, voice-controlled VCRs and command-controlled factory machinery. The query terms of command controlled devices tend to be fixed, allowing more application-specific information to be incorporated into the keyword detection process. The device includes query word linguistic context information and environmental noise conditions.

Hence, command controlled device keyword spotting lends itself to the development of custom solutions. Though many of these solutions may be based on existing keyword spotting approaches, significant enhancements and modifications are made to provide maximum performance for the intended application.

Dialogue System

Automated dialogue systems are becoming more common in the commercial environment as a viable alternative to human-operated call centers. A dialogue system mimics a human call-centre operator by playing voice prompts to a caller and then attempting to detect keywords that indicate the response of the caller. Since the volume of calls processed by a call centre can be very large, STT approaches are infeasible due to their high computational requirements. Keyword spotting technologies are used to interpret the response of the callers.

1.7. General Framework of Keyword Spotting System

A general framework of the standard keyword spotting system is described in the Figure 1.3. The keyword spotting system consists of two main stages: training and template matching. Before the spotting work, acoustic feature parameters are extracted from each consecutive speech segments of a given spoken content and the specified keyword. During the training stage, a training vector is generated from the speech signal of each word spoken by the user. The training vectors extract the spectral features for distinguishing different classes of words. Each training vector can serve as a template for a single word or a word class. These feature vectors are stored in a database for subsequent use in the template matching phase.

The template matching phase identifies the keyword uttered by the user by matching it with the trained templates. Feature vector is generated for that word and compared with the trained templates using pattern matching algorithm. The similarity score determined by the pattern matching algorithm is used to decide the occurrence of the keyword in the speech content.

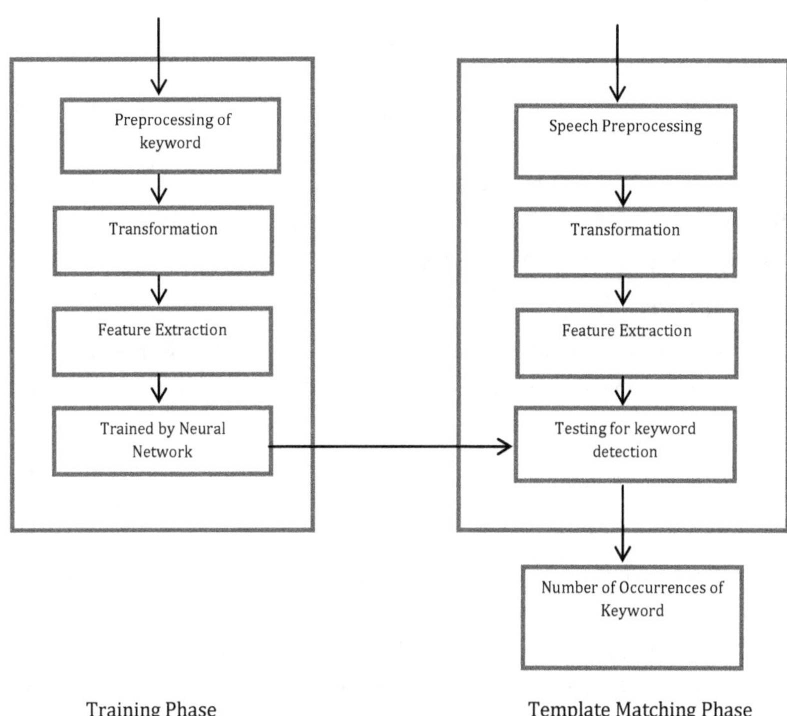

Figure 1.3: General Framework of Keyword Spotting System

1.8. Keyword Spotting Technologies

The keyword spotting system analyzes a given spoken content segment by segment and locates the predefined keywords. Most of the works on keyword spotting are based on Hidden Markov models. Besides, there are some methods that are independent of Hidden Markov models. Keywords are important for carrying out the basic concepts of speech; and the meaning of speech. There are three main approaches to identify the keywords. The most obvious approach is to use a large vocabulary continuous speech recognition system to produce a word string, and then to search for the keyword in this word string.

1.8.1. LVCSR KWS

In LVCSR KWS, the entire test audio data is first transcribed into text and then the text transcription is used for searching the keywords. Hence LVCSR KWS is a two-step process. In the first phase, this method converts speech into text and in the second phase, it identifies keywords in the generated dictionary that can contain several hundred thousand entries. If the keyword is not in the dictionary, the system will choose the most similar word it can find. LVCSR systems are more complex and expensive to implement [A. Moyal et al, 2013].

Although a keyword search that is implemented on fully transcribedtext in the LVCSR method is fast (particularly if the text has also been indexed), it isusually at a disadvantage in comparison to the phonetic search and acousticmethods due to the fact that an LVCSR engine demands a large vocabulary and acomplex language model to produce recognition results, thus resulting in a highlevel of complexity during the pre-processing stage.

1.8.2. Acoustic KWS

Acoustic KWS does not attempt to transcribe the entire stream of speech. In acoustic KWS, the keyword search can be performed directly from untranscribed audio stream.

Speech signals are represented as bark based energy or mel scale coefficients or they are represented as phoneme posterior grams generated by an acoustic model. This acoustic KWS can be performed in only one stage. This approach is easy to implement and provides some pronunciation tolerance.

The acoustic based KWS uses a vocabulary consisting only of the keywords and does not require a language model at all. Because the acoustic-based method operates on the speech itself and requires only a small vocabulary, it is appropriate for real-time keyword spotting or KWS in small speech databases. However, this means that general speech must be well-modeled (Thambiratnam, 2005) to avoid extensive over detection.

1.8.3. Phonetic KWS

Phonetic KWS is phoneme based indexing method. This method doesn't convert speech into text but divides it into phonemes. Phonetic KWS is also a two-step process. In the first step, audio is processed (indexed) with a phonetic recognizer to generate a phonetic index file. In second step, system uses the generated dictionary of phonemes to compare the user's search term to the correct phonetic string. This approach combines the advantages of the LVCSR based keyword spotting and acoustic keyword spotting. The phonetic search method performs phoneme recognition using phoneme transition probabilities (di-phones) with no lexicon or word level language model. During the search stage, however, phonetic search KWS uses a textual sequencedistance measure that requires more computation. This is because the phonetic search must generate word-level hypotheses based on phoneme sequences; while inLVCSR-based KWS the textual output is already word-level.

1.9. KWS Approaches

1.9.1. Pattern Matching Approach

Dynamic Time Warping (DTW) Approach

DTW is a dynamic programming technique used for measuring the similarity between any two time series with arbitrary lengths. The time alignment of different utterances is the core problem for distance measurement in speech recognition. A small shift leads to incorrect identification. DTW algorithm aims at aligning two sequences of feature vectors by warping the time axis repetitively until an optimal match between the two sequences is found. To align both the signals, this algorithm does a section wise linear mapping of the time axis.

The DTW approach is based on comparing a keyword template with a segment of speech. Firstly, features are extracted from both the keyword and the utterance. Existing work has shown that Mel Frequency Cepstral Coefficients (MFCCs) are one of the best features [Jansen A. and Niyogi P, 2009] and hence are used as spectral features. Then, the extracted feature vectors AM and BN from the template and the utterance are compared and a match is indicated when the distance measured between the templates is below a threshold. Such approaches generally require training to determine the appropriate threshold. The approach used here depends on a hypothesis that the distance between the word template and sections of the utterance that do not contain the word is high compared with the distance resulting from comparing the template with parts of the utterance that contain the word [Barakat, 2000].

Segmental Dynamic Warping Algorithm (SDTW)

Segmental DTW is a variant of traditional dynamic time warping which searches for multiple local alignments of two input utterances, X and Y, and their associated distance matrix D. The algorithm works by dividing the distance matrix into a set of diagonal bands of width R and searching for the best warp path within each band.

The diagonal bands serve multiple purposes. First, they constrain the degree of warping so that two sub-utterances are not overly temporally distorted during alignment. Second, they allow for multiple alignments, as each band corresponds to another potential path with different start and end points.

SDTW compromises of two main components: a local alignment procedure which produces multiple warp paths that have limited temporal variation, and a path trimming procedure which retains only the lower distortion regions of an alignment path. The major modification over traditional DTW for this implementation is the imposition of two constraints. The first one is the adjustment window constraint to restrict the shapes that a warping path can take as already defined in the previous section in the report. Second, multiple alignment paths are allowed for the same two input sequences by employing different starting and ending points in traditional DTW search algorithm.

1.9.2. *Hidden Markov Model (HMM) Approach*

Hidden Markov Model is a statistical model in which the system is assumed to be a Markov process with unobservable states. The output of each state however is observable and each state has a probability distribution over the possible outcomes. HMM are most widely used for speech recognition as well as keyword spotting. Assuming the speech signal to be piecewise stationary, each word is modeled as a sequence of stationary units with a certain set of acoustic feature parameters. Although there are several linguistic arguments for choosing units such as syllable or semi-syllable, the unit most commonly used is the phoneme. Isolated word recognition using HMM models can be broken down into two steps.

   i.   For each word in the vocabulary, build an HMM, i.e., estimate the model parameters that optimizes the likelihood of the training set.

   ii.   Observation sequence is obtained for each word to be recognized by feature extraction and likelihood for all possible models is calculated. The word with highest likelihood is selected as a match. This is done using the Viterbi algorithm to optimize the computation.

For large vocabulary continuous speech recognition (LVSCR), syntactical models are also used along with the word model to apply grammatical constraints. This additional linguistic constraint makes the recognition task easier and also increases the performance of the system. A simple form of the two states KWS can be directly implemented using Large Vocabulary Continuous Speech Recognizer (LVSCR). But this requires training the model for a large dictionary of words and huge language model which is rather impractical.

An alternative approach is to consider the speech signal to be composed to keywords and non-keywords and using garbage or filler models to characterize non-keywords. Some systems add extra models for representing non-speech events such as silence or coughing. Both the keyword model and the garbage model are built from a concatenation of phoneme sub-models.

Likelihood of test utterance matching the keyword model gives the confidence measure of detection of the keyword.

1.9.3. Other Approaches

The HMM approach requires a large amount of supervised training data, i.e., data that are manually segmented and labeled. The HMM based statistical approach favors the most occurring events because they aim at maximizing the likelihood of an event, but the keywords of interested might not be available in abundance. Moreover, HMM based systems are difficult to train in other languages because of the lack of transcribed data [Hazen, et al. 2009]. They are also known for poorly modeling long temporal dependencies, which needs to be circumvented with refined features or adaptation techniques [Grangier, et al. 2007]. In order to overcome these issues, significant effort has been made towards improving template based recognition and discriminative approaches to keyword spotting [Keshet, et al. 2009].

Other methods based on Neural Network are also used for speech recognition. Besides the methods discussed above, there are other methods based on Support Vector Machines SVM [Keshet, et al. 2009], iterative clustering and Self organizing Maps and Learning Vector Quantization [Somervuo, et al. 1999], hybrid methods combining two or more methods are also used for keyword spotting [Morgan, et al. 1990]. Besides slight increases of the performance by few points percentage, none of the methods have significantly outperformed original HMM despite tremendous increase in computation.

Most of the existing KWS approaches are in relation to template matching that use some sort of variations in DTW. An unsupervised learning framework to address the problem of audio keyword spotting is presented by [Bahi, H., and Benati, N, 2009]. Without any transcription of information, a Gaussian mixture model (GMM) is trained to represent each speech frame with a Gaussian posteriorgram. A segmental dynamic time warping (SDTW) technique is used to compare the Gaussian posteriorgrams between keyword examples and unseen test data. It uses the HMMs for posteriorgrams representation that may take a huge amount of computational cost. A keyword spotter presented in [Bahi, H., and Benati, N, 2009] used MFCC and energy of the speech signal as feature set. The Vector Quantization (VQ) algorithm is used for codebook generation. The HMMs are used for the probability assignment for observation of given a word. This system is based on VQ and HMM that need a high computational time for training the learning models.

A new word spotting approach in continuous speech is introduced in [Khan w., 2014] that use wavelet transform based feature extraction and Euclidean distance. The system is capable of identifying and localizing a target word in a continuous speech of any length. A neural

Network based method for keyword spotting is addressed in [Jothilakshmi, S., 2013]. The work concerns the use of the distribution capturing ability of the Auto Associative Neural Network (AANN) for spoken keyword detection. It involves sliding a frame-based keyword template along the speech signal and using confidence score obtained from the normalized squared error of AANN to efficiently search for a match.

CHAPTER 2

SPEECH SIGNAL PROCESSING

2.1. Introduction

Speech is the most natural form of human communication and speech processing has been one of the most exciting research areas of the signal processing [X. Huang and L. Deng, 2010]. Speech processing is the study of speech signals and the processing methods of these signals. The signals are usually processed in a digital representation, so speech processing can be regarded as a special case of digital signal processing, applied to speech signal. It is a unique discipline which encompasses a broad range and a variety of technologies and applications.

Speech processing refers to analysis and processing of speech signals with the aim to achieve maximum benefit in various practical scenarios like information retrieval or speaker recognition. Since the signals are usually processed in digital form, speech processing can be placed at the confluence of digital signal processing and natural language processing.

Automation of speech processing is of great importance in practical applications where the human factor is involved only in the final stage of interpreting and using the processing results.

2.1.1. Research Directions in Speech

The speech processing covers a broad area that relates to the following important research directions:

- **Speech recognition:** analysis of the linguistic content of the speech signal.
- **Speaker recognition:** checks the identity of the speaker from speech signal.
- **Speech signal enhancement:** focuses on quality aspects of the speech signal.
- **Speech coding:** specialized form of data compression.
- **Voice analysis:** deals with medical purposes, such as analysis of vocal loading and dysfunction of vocal cords.
- **Speech synthesis:** artificial synthesis of speech.
- **Keyword Spotting:** Monitoring the occurrences of the predefined keyword

A comprehensive state-of-the-art research of the techniques in robust speech processing have been motivated by the increase of the need for low-complexity and efficient speech feature extraction methods, the need for enhancing the naturalness, acceptability and intelligibility of the received speech signal corrupted by environmental noise, and the need of reducing noise for robust speech recognition systems to achieve high recognition rate in harsh environments.

2.1.2. *Applications of Speech Processing*

The applications of speech processing are mostly useful in day to day life of people. Some of the speech processing applications are Speech Coding, Text-to-Speech Synthesis, Speech Recognition, Speaker Recognition and Verification, Keyword Spotting, Speech Enhancement, Speech Segmentation and Labeling (Transcription), Language Identification, Prosody, Attitude and Emotion recognition, Audio-Visual Signal Processing and Spoken Dialog Systems.

2.2. Speech Signals

The human voice consists of sound made by a human being using the vocal folds for talking, singing, laughing, crying, screaming, etc. Its frequency ranges from about 60 to 7000 Hz. The human voice is specifically that part of human sound production in which the vocal folds (vocal cords) are the primary sound source. Generally speaking, the mechanism for generating the human voice can be subdivided into three parts; the lungs, the vocal folds within the larynx, and the articulators, e.g. tongue, palate, cheeks and lips. In telephony, the usable voice frequency band ranges from approximately 300 Hz to 3400 Hz. The bandwidth allocated for a single voice-frequency transmission channel is usually 4 kHz, including guard bands.

2.2.1. *Characteristics of Speech Signals*

Normal and good speech signalspossess the following characteristics:

Quality of Voice: In a quality voice, the number of harmonious noise ratio should be 15.

Pitch: Pitch is the psychological co-relate of frequency. Pitch should not be too high, too low, and monotonous or stereotype.

Loudness: The loudness of the speakershould be normal i.e. in the range of 40-80 dB.

Intonation: Intonation means variation of pitch or fluctuation of pitch during the delivery of the speech. Normal male adult and female should have the pitch range of one and a half and two octave respectively.

Rate of Speech: Rate of speech refers to the number of words or syllables uttered in a particular time period. Speaker's rate of speech should be 140 words and 300 syllables per minute or 2.5 words and 7 syllables per second. Being too fast may result in omission of syllable and articulation may not be similar.

Rhythm: Rhythm refers to easy and smooth flow or continuity of speech. A spontaneous flow of speech that can be observed during its delivery is to be devoid of implements, repetitions, hesitations, pauses or stops in syllables. Stuttering mars the beauty of rhythm.

Stress: Stress refers to extra pressure given on a particular syllable during speech. Appropriate use of stress makes the speech an effective one.

Articulation: The process of production of single speech sound is called Articulation. Speaker should utter properly. Intelligibility of speech depends on proper articulation.

Intelligibility of Speech: High intelligibility possesses good speech.

Flexibility: Flexibility is one of the most important characteristics of speech. Speech should be flexible depending on situations. Flexibility of speech depends on the manner of its deliverance.

2.2.2. Speech File Formats

An audio file format is a file format for storing digital audio data on a computer system. The bit layout of the audio data is called the audio coding format and can be compressed to reduce the file size, often using lossy compression. The data can be a raw bit stream in an audio coding format, but it is usually embedded in a container format or an audio data format with defined storage layer. There are three major groups of audio file formats:

- Uncompressed audio formats
- Formats with lossless compression
- Formats with lossy compression

Uncompressed Audio Formats

One major uncompressed audio format, LPCM, is the format most commonly accepted by low level audio. Although LPCM can be stored on a computer as a raw audio format, it is usually stored in a .wav file on Windows. The WAV format is based on the similar Resource Interchange File Format (RIFF). WAV is not inherently lossless; it is designed to store a wide variety of audio formats, lossless and lossy. Since WAV is widely supported and can store LPCM, it is the most suitable file format for storing and archiving an original recording.

Formats with Lossless Compression

A lossless compressed format stores data in less space with no loss of any information. The original, uncompressed data can be recreated from the compressed version. Uncompressed audio formats encode both sound and silence with the same number of bits per unit of time. Encoding an uncompressed minute of absolute silence produces a file of the same size as encoding an uncompressed minute of music. In a lossless compressed format, however, the music would occupy a smaller file than an uncompressed format and the silence would take up almost no space at all.

Formats with Lossy Compression

Lossy compression enables even greater reductions in file size by the removal some of the audio information and simplification of the data. It also results in a reduction in audio quality, but a variety of techniques are used, mainly to remove the parts of the sound that have the least effect on perceived quality, and to minimize the amount of audible noise added during the process. Most compression is generally measured in terms of bit rate.

2.3.   Types of Speech Signals

Speech processing systems can be classified into several different classes by describing what types of utterances they could process. The following are the classifications [M.A.Anusuya and S.K.Katti, 2009]:

2.3.1.   Isolated Words

Isolated word recognizers usually require each utterance to be silent(lack of an audio signal) on both sides of the sample window. It accepts single word or an utterance at a time. Isolated Utterance might be a better name for this class.An isolated-word system operates on single words at a time and requires a pause between words. This is the simplest form of recognition to perform because the end points are easier to find and the pronunciation of a word tends not to affect others. Thus, because the occurrences of words are consistent they are easier for processing.

2.3.2.   Connected Words

Connected words are speech data that is spoken with pauses between words to make it easier for a computer to recognize. Connected word systems (or more correctly 'connected utterances') are similar to isolated words, but allows separate utterances to run-together with a minimal pause between them.

2.3.3.   Continuous Speech

Continuous speech is spoken without pauses between words. In continuous speech, users are allowed to speak almost naturally, while the computer determines the content.Speech recognizers of continuous speech capabilities are most difficult to be created because they utilize special methods to determine utterance boundaries. A continuous speech system operates on speech in which words are connected together, i.e. not separated by pauses. Continuous speech is more difficult to handle because of a variety of reasons. First, it is difficult to find the first and final points of words. Another problem is co-articulation. The production of each phoneme is affected by the production of surrounding phonemes, and similarly the beginning and end of words are affected by the preceding and following words. The recognition of continuous speech is also affected by the rate of speech.

2.3.4. Spontaneous Speech

Spontaneous speech can be thought of as a speech thatsoundsnatural and not rehearsed. A speech processing system with spontaneous speech ability should be able to handle a variety of natural speech features such as words being run together, "ums" and "ahs", and even slight stutters.

2.4.   Speech Signal Analysis

2.4.1. Speech Acoustics

Speech Waves

Speech signal is sinusoidal signal with different frequencies, different amplitudes and phases.

It is represented by the following expression:

$$\sum_{i-1}^{N} A_i(t)\sin\left[2\pi F_i(t)t+\theta_i(t)\right] \quad (2.1)$$

where, A_i (t), F_i (t) & θ_i (t) are the sets of amplitudes, frequencies & phases respectively, of the sinusoids. An example for a sinusoidal signal is shown in Figure 2.1.

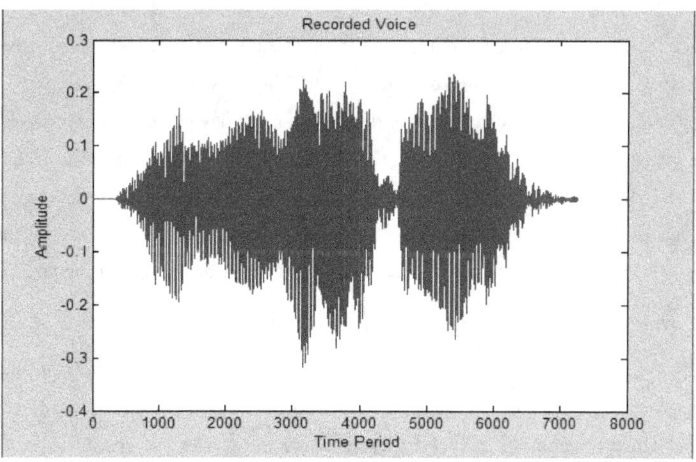

Figure 2.1: Plot of a Sinusoidal Signal

Frequency

Frequency is related to the individual pulsations produced by vocal cord vibrations for a unit of time. The rate of vibration depends on the length, thickness, and tension of the vocal cords, and thus is different for a child and an adult male and a female speech. A speech sound contains two types of frequencies: fundamental frequency (F0) which is related to vocal cord function and which reflects the rate of vocal cord vibration during phonation (pitch) and formant frequency which is related to vocal tract configuration.

Amplitude

Amplitude is directly related to the acoustic energy or intensity of a sound. The amplitude of the vibrations (i.e. the size of the oscillations of the vocal folds) affects the loudness. The greater the amplitude of the vibrations, the greater the amount of energy carried by the wave. The amplitude is marked by darkness of the bands: the greater the intensity of the sound energy presents in a given time and frequency, the darker will be the mark at the corresponding point on the screen.

Formant

A formant is a concentration of acoustic energy around a particular frequency in the speech wave. There are several formants, each at a different frequency, roughly one in each 1000Hz band. Each formant corresponds to a resonance in the vocal tract.

Spectrogram

A spectrogram is a visual representation of the spectrum of frequencies in a sound or other signal as they vary with time or some other variable. It is a representation of how the frequency content of a signal changes with time. Time is displayed along the x-axis, frequency alongthe y-axis, and the amount of energy in the signal at any given time and frequency is displayed as a level of grey. During regions of silence, and at frequency regions where there is little energy, the spectrogram appears white; dark regions indicate areas of energy caused, for example, by vocal fold closures, harmonious, or formant vibration in a speech signal

2.4.2.   Drawbacks in Speech Processing

Speech contains not only irrelevant words but also non-intentional sounds likecough, exclamations and noise. In addition, people do not speak interms of isolated words; there are no distinct word boundaries in speech, which make the process of speech more difficult. Moreover, there is always some variation in a word every time it isuttered even by the same person. It is shown in the figure 2.2. Thus a number of challenging technologies are to be emerged for speech processing.

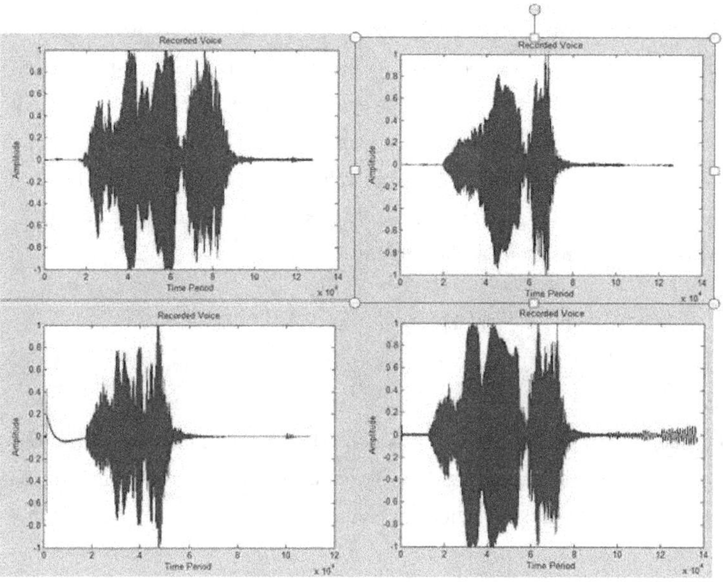

Figure 2.2: Plot of Four Instances of the Word "Ondru" by the Same Speaker

2.4.3. *Voiced and Unvoiced Speech*

A typical speech sentence signal consists of two main parts: one carries the speech information, and the other includes silent or noise sections that are between the utterances, without any verbal information. The verbal (informative) part of speech can be further divided into two categories: voiced and unvoiced speech.

Voiced Speech

Voiced speech consists mainly of vowel sounds. It is produced by forcing air through the glottis.Proper adjustment of the tension of the vocal cords results in opening and closing of the cords, producing of almost periodicpulses of air. These pulses excite the vocal tract and hold most of the information of the speech and thus keep the keys for characterizing a speaker.

Unvoiced Speech

Unvoiced speech sections are generated by forcing air through a constriction formed at a point in the vocal tract (usually toward the mouth end), thus producing turbulence.

2.4.4. Voiced/Unvoiced Determination Features

Zero Crossing Rate

The rate at which the speech signal crosses zero can provide information about the source of its creation. The unvoiced speech has a much higher ZCR than voiced speech [L. R. Rabiner, R. W. Schafer]. This is because most of the energy in unvoiced speech is found with higher frequencies than in voiced speech, implying a higher ZCR for the former. As shown in the figure 2.3, in voiced speech, the short-time energy values are much higher than that in unvoiced speech, which has a higher zero crossing rate. A possible definition for the ZCR [L. R. Rabiner , R. W. Schafer] is presented in the following equation:

$$w(n) = \frac{1}{2N} \quad 0<=n<=N\text{-}1 \quad (2.2)$$

Energy

The amplitude of unvoiced segments is noticeably lower than that of the voiced segments. Theshort-time energy of speech signals reflects the amplitude variation and is defined [L. R. Rabiner and R. W. Schafer] in equation represented below.

$$E_n = \sum_{m=-\alpha}^{\alpha} x^2(m).h(n-m)$$

In order to reflect the amplitude variations in time (for this a short window is necessary), and considering the need for a low pass filter to provide smoothing, h(n) is chosen to be a hamming window powered by 2. It has been shown to give good results in terms of reflecting amplitude variations.

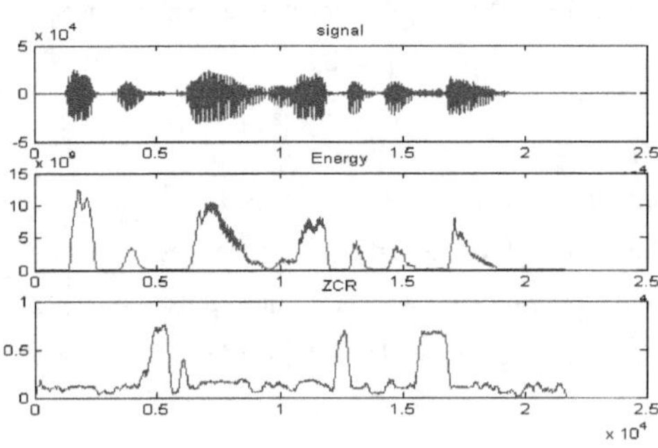

Figure 2.3: Plot of a Speech Signal with its Short-time Energy and Zero Crossing Rate

[L. R. Rabiner]

Cross-correlation

Cross-correlation is calculated between two consecutive pitch cycles. The cross-correlation values between pitch cycles are higher (close to 1) in voiced speech than in unvoiced speech.

$$Corr = \sum_{i=0}^{N-1} \sum_{j=0}^{N-1} P_{i,j} \left[\frac{(i-\mu_i)(j-\mu_j)}{\sqrt{\sigma_i^2 \sigma_j^2}} \right] \qquad (2.3)$$

Pitch Detection

Voiced speech signals can be considered as quasi-periodic. The basic period is called the pitch period. The average pitch frequency (in short, the pitch), time pattern, gain, and fluctuation change from one speaker to another. For speech signal analysis, and especially for synthesis, identifying the pitch is extremely important.

A well-known method for pitch detection is given in [Yoav Meden et al, 1991]. It is based on the fact that two consecutive pitch cycles have a high cross-correlation value, as opposed to two consecutive speech fractions of the same length but different from the pitch cycle time. The pitch detection can be represented by the following equations:

$$\langle x, y \rangle = \int_{t_0}^{t_0+z} x(t).y(t)\,dt \; ; \, y(t) = x(t-\tau) \qquad (2.4)$$

$$T_0 = \arg\max(\rho_z); \; \rho_z = \frac{\langle x, y \rangle}{\| x \| . \| y \|} ; \; \| x \| = \left(\langle x, x \rangle \right)^{1/2} \qquad (2.5)$$

2.5. Speech Pre-processing Techniques

Pre-processing is an important and critical step in the mining process and it has a huge impact on the success of a speech mining research. The preprocessing stage in speech processing is used in order to increase the efficiency of subsequent feature extraction and classification stages and therefore to improve the overall performance of the method. Commonly, the preprocessing includes the sampling, denoising, framing and windowing. At the end of the preprocessing the compressed and filtered speech frames are forwarded to the feature extraction stage. The general preprocessing pipeline is depicted in the following figure 2.4.

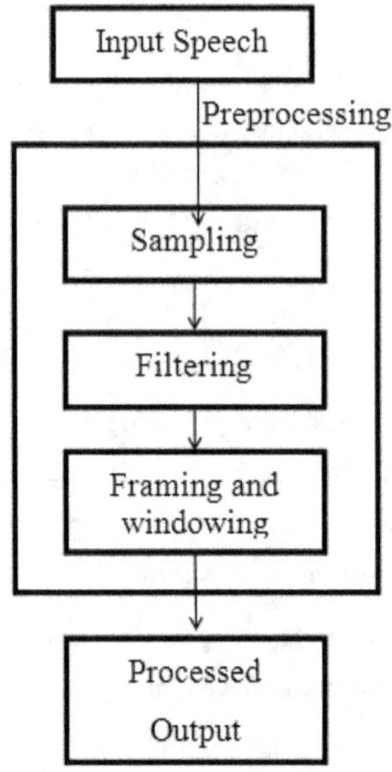

Figure 2.4: General Steps of the Preprocessing Stage

2.5.1. Sampling

In order that a computer is able to process the speech signal, it first has to be digitized. Therefore the time-continuous speech signal is sampled and quantized. The result is a time and value discrete signal. Usually, speech processing systems encode the samples with 8 or 16 bits per sample depending on the available processing power. A signal is considered to be stationary if its frequency or spectral components do not change over time. In order to obtain frames the speech signal has to be multiplied with a windowing function. This windowing function weighs the signal in the time domain and divides it into a sequence of partial signals.

2.5.2. Noise Reduction

The stage of denoising or noise reduction aims to improve the quality of speech signals. The objective is to improve the intelligibility, a measure to find comprehensible a speech is. Noise corrupting speech signals can be grouped into the following 3 classes:

- Noise creation by Microphone
- Electrical noise
- Environmental noise

The first two types of noise can be easily compensated by training the speech recognizers on corresponding noisy speech samples, but compensating the environmental noise is not that elementary due to its high variability. The basic problem of noise reduction is to reduce the environmental noise without disturbing the speech signal.

2.5.3. *Filtering*

In signal processing, a filter is a process that removes the unwanted component of the signal. Analysis of data is a very important task since it is the source of information whichwill be fed into the certain techniques, namely, classification or prediction. Thepresence of noise often leads to a wrong interpretation of the data. Therefore, aninitial platform is needed for data denoising process. Filtering can be one of denoising platform for time series data and it is an indispensable task to deal with [Ghosh & Raychaudhuri, 2007].

Filtering is the process of defining, detecting and correcting errors in given data, in order to minimize the impact of errors in input data on succeeding analyses [Wedin et al., 2008].There are several filters commonly used in research to separate the behavior of the time series.Digital filters can be classified into two categories and they are the Finite Impulse Response (FIR) filter and Infinite Impulse Response (IIR) filter [Datar et al, 2009]. In the FIR system, the impulse response is of finite duration, which means that it has a finite number of nonzero terms [Yu-Chi Tsao et al, 2012]. On the other hand, The IIR system has an infinite number of nonzero terms. This means that its impulse response is of infinite duration. The structure of FIR filter is much more simpler when compared to that of the IIR filter [Soni et al, 2011] [Sanal M. et al, 2013]. Generally by applying Fourier series method, Frequency sampling method or Window method, the FIR filter can be obtained [Mehboob et al, 2009].

FIR filter types are classified into four types. They are:

- Low pass filters
- High pass filters
- Band pass filters
- Band stop filters

Low–Pass Filter

Low–Pass Filter (LPF) is an electronic filter that passes low frequency signals butattenuates signals with frequencies higher than the cutoff frequency [Thomas et al, 2000]. The actual amount of attenuation for each frequency varies from filter to filter.It is sometimes called a high cut filter. A low pass filter is the opposite of a high passfilter.

High–Pass Filter

High–Pass Filter (HPF) passes high frequency signals but attenuates signals with frequencies lower than the cutoff frequency. A high pass filteris usually modeled as a linear time invariant system. It is sometimes called a low cutfilter or bass cut filter. It can also be used in conjunction with a lowpass filter to make a band pass filter.

Band–Pass Filter

A Band–Pass Filter (BPF) is a filter that passes frequencies within a certain rangeand rejects frequencies outside that range. It passes a suitable frequency band that is required for desired applications. An analogue electronic band pass filter is a resistorinductor capacitor circuit. This filter can also be created by combining a low passfilter with a high pass filter [Anderson *et al.*, 2012].

Band–Stop Filter

The Band Stop Filter (BSF) is another type of frequency filter that functions in exactly the opposite way to the Band Pass Filter. The band stop filter, also known as a band reject filter, passes all frequencies with the exception of those within a specified stop band which are greatly attenuated. However, among all the fourfiltering techniques, the wavelet approach has shown some advantages over theconventional filtering techniques. Some of the conventional filtering techniques are discussed below.

Adaptive Filter

Adaptive Filter is to obtain an estimate of the noise signal and subtract it from the corrupted signal. The adaptive noise cancellation technique uses adaptive filters for signal processing. This filter is a popular one in many signal enhancement methods. The basic idea of this filter is to obtain estimate of speech signal from the corrupted signal particularly by additive noise. This estimate is calculated by minimizing the Mean Square Error (MSE) between the desired signals.

Moving Average Filter

The Moving Average (MA) filter is a simple Low Pass FIR (Finite Impulse Response) filter commonly used for smoothing an array of sampled signal. It takes M samples of input at a time and take the average of those M-samples and produces a single output point.As the lengthof the filter increases, the smoothness of the output increases, whereas the sharp transitions in the signal are made increasingly blunt. This implies that this filter has excellent time domain but a poor frequency response.The moving average filter takes average samples for filtering the noise from signal [J. G. Proakis and D. G. Manolakis, 2004]. The expression of output of such filter is given below.

$$Y(n) = \frac{X(n) + X(n-1) + X(n-2)}{3} \quad (2.6)$$

where, X(n)is the input speech sample.This Moving average filters which are implemented by magnitude & phase [Syed Mohammad Ali. et al, 2013] are more stable.

2.5.4. *Framing and Windowing*

Human speech signal is slowly varies over time that is when it is examined over a short period of time. The signal is fairly stationary. Therefore speech signals are often analyzed in short time segments which are referred to as short term spectral analysis. This practically means that the signal is blocked in frames of typically 20-30 msec. Adjacent frames typically overlap each other with 30% to 50 %. This is done in order not to lose any information due to the windowing. Human speech signal also slowly varies over time and can be treated as stationary process when considered under a short time frame. Therefore, the speech signal is usually separated into small duration blocks called frames. The neighborhood blocks are overlapped by 1/2 to 2/3 length of the frame & frame shift is frame length minus the frame overlap. The commonly used frame length & frame shifts are 20 to 30m sec & 10m sec respectively.

Windowing Techniques

Window technique implies a function called window function. It is also known as tapering function. It states that if some interval is chosen, it returns with finite non-zero value inside that interval and zero value outside that interval. A major effect of windowing is that the discontinuities of the frequency response are converted into transition bands between values on either side of the discontinuity.

There are many window techniques available for designing the FIR filter and they are [Bob Meddins, 2000] [Ramesh .R, and Nathiya .R, 2012][P. Ramesh Babu, 2008] [Andreas Antoniou, 2006]:

- Hanning window
- Hamming window
- Blackman window
- Rectangular window
- Bartlett window
- Kaiser window etc.

The Hamming window sequence can be defined by the following equation [Magatha Nayak Bhukya et al, 2012]:

$$w(n) = \alpha - \beta \cos\left(\frac{2\pi n}{N-1}\right) \text{ for } -\frac{N-1}{2} \leq n \leq \frac{N-1}{2} \quad (2.7)$$

With α= 0.54 β=1 - α=0.46

The window function of a causal Hanning window [Manoj Garg et al, 2010] is expressed by,

$$W_{hann(n)} = \{0.5 - 0.5\cos\frac{2\pi n}{N-1}, 0 \leq n \leq N-1 \; ; 0, \text{ otherwise} \quad (2.8)$$

The figure 2.5 shows the outputs of four different filters with Hamming window [Prajoy Podder, 2014].

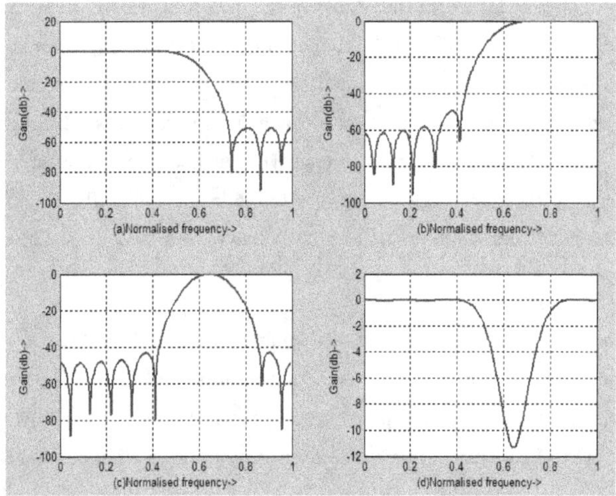

Figure 2.5: Filters Using Hamming Window (a) Low Pass (b) High Pass (c) Band Pass (d) Band Stop [Prajoy Podder, 2014]

2.6.   Discussion

Speech processing is the study of speech signals and the processing methods of these signals. Automation of speech processing is of great importance in practical applications where the human factor is involved only in the final stage of interpreting and using the processing results. Various speech characteristics and file formats are discussed. Speech signals are classified as isolated words, connected words, continuous speech and spontaneous speech. Depending on the types of the signals, various speech processing are applied.

Speech preprocessing tasks framing, sampling and filtering are discussed. Filtering is one of the preprocessing tasks that removes the unwanted component of the signal. Different type of filters are used in speech preprocessing. Various keyword spotting approaches have been developed. The approaches are based on DTW algorithm, SDTW algorithm, HMM, VQ, Neural Network and other approaches. The existing related works are discussed.

CHAPTER 3

WAVELET TRANSFORMATION OF SPEECH SIGNALS

3.1.   Introduction

The transform of a signal is just another form of representing the signal. It does not change the information content present in the signal. Signals are categorized into two types: Stationary signals and non-stationary signals. A stationary signal doesn't change much over the time. However, most interesting signals are non-stationary that contains numerous transitory characteristics: drift, trends, abrupt changes, and beginnings and ends of events. These characteristics are often the most important part of the signal, and Fourier analysis is not suited to detecting them and Fourier analysis is not suited to detecting them.

The development of the wavelet transform (WT) is considered a revolution of modern signal processing techniques and most widely used over the past two decades. The Wavelet Transform provides a time-frequency representation of the signal. Significant contributions of wavelet analysis to different signal processing techniques have been developed for signal, image and speech processing as well as applications.

A major advantage of wavelet transform is the simultaneous representation of time and frequency analysis which helps to filter out the noisy segments from the spectrum as well as from the time domain speech sign al. Wavelet decomposition analyses the function at various levels of resolution and provides a simultaneous time-frequency representation of input speech signal. This representation empowers the wavelet's superiority because of its efficiency for localizing the frequency in time domain along with the correlation matrix as a third dimension. Approximation and detailed coefficients possessing the magnitude values below the threshold are filtered out while remaining coefficients are integrated together and forwarded for further processing.

3.2.   Speech Transformation

To extract information from speech signals and reveal the underlying dynamics that corresponds to the signals, proper signal processing technique is needed. Typically, the process of signal processing transforms a time-domain signal into another domain, with the purpose of extracting the characteristic information embedded within the signal that is otherwise not readily observable in its original form. Mathematically, this can be achieved by representing the time-domain signal as a series of coefficients, based on a comparison between the signal x (t) and a set of known, template functions $\{\Psi_n(t)\} n \in z$ as [Chui 1992; Qian 2002]

$$C_n = \int_{-\infty}^{\infty} x(t)\psi_n(t)dt \quad (3.1)$$

where $(\cdot)^*$ stands for the complex conjugate of the function $(\cdot)$. The inner product between the two functions $x(t)$ and $\psi_n(t)$ is defined as

$$\langle x,\psi_n \rangle = \int_{-\infty}^{\infty} x(t)\psi_n(t)dt \quad (3.2)$$

Then (3.1) can be expressed in the general form as

$$C_n = \langle x,\psi_n \rangle \quad (3.3)$$

3.2.1. *Fourier Transform*

The Fourier transform is the most widely applied signal processing tool in science and engineering. It reveals the frequency composition of a time series x (t) by transforming it from the time domain into the frequency domain. In 1807, the French mathematician Joseph Fourier [1822], found that any periodic signal can be presented by a weighted sum of a series of sine and cosine functions. The Fourier transform of a signal x (t) can be expressed as

$$X(f) = \langle x,e^{i2\pi ft} \rangle = \int_{-\infty}^{\infty} x(t)e^{i2\pi ft}dt \quad (3.4)$$

Assuming that the signal has finite energy,

$$\int_{-\infty}^{\infty} |x(t)|^2 \, dt < \infty \quad (3.5)$$

Accordingly, the inverse Fourier transform of the signal x (t) can be expressed as

$$x(t) = \int_{-\infty}^{\infty} X(f)e^{i2\pi ft}df \quad (3.6)$$

Signals obtained experimentally through a data acquisition system are generally sampled at discrete time intervals ΔT, instead of continuously, within a total measurement time T. Such a signal, defined as x_k, can be transformed into the frequency domain by using the discrete Fourier transform (DFT), defined as

$$DFT(f_n) = \frac{1}{N}\sum_{k=0}^{N-1} x_k e^{-i2\pi f_n k\Delta T} \quad (3.7)$$

where N=T/ΔT is the number of samples, and f_n =1/T; n =0 1, 2, . . . , N -1 are the discrete frequency components. The inverse DFT can then be expressed as

$$x_k = \frac{1}{\Delta T} \sum_{f_n=0}^{(N-1)/T} DFT(f_n)e^{i2\pi f_n}k\Delta T \qquad (3.8)$$

Cooley–Tukey algorithm which is also called the fast Fourier transform (FFT) [Cooley and Tukey 1965], and what it does is to recursively break down a DFT of a large data sample (i.e., a large N) into a series of smaller DFTs of smaller samples by dividing the transform with size N into two pieces of size N/2 at each step, and reduce the arithmetic operations to a total of N log(N).

Fourier Transform does not reveal how the signal's frequency contents vary with time. Because the temporal structure of the signal is not revealed, the merit of the Fourier transform is limited; specifically, it is not suited for analyzing non-stationary signals. Thus a new signal processing technique that is able to handle the non-stationary of a signal is needed.

3.2.2. Short-Time Fourier Transform

A straight forward solution to overcoming the limitations of the Fourier transform is to introduce an analysis window of certain length that glides through the signal along the time axis to perform a "time-localized" Fourier transform. Such a concept led to the short-time Fourier transform (STFT) [Gabor, 1946].STFT maps a signal into a two-dimensional function of time and frequency.

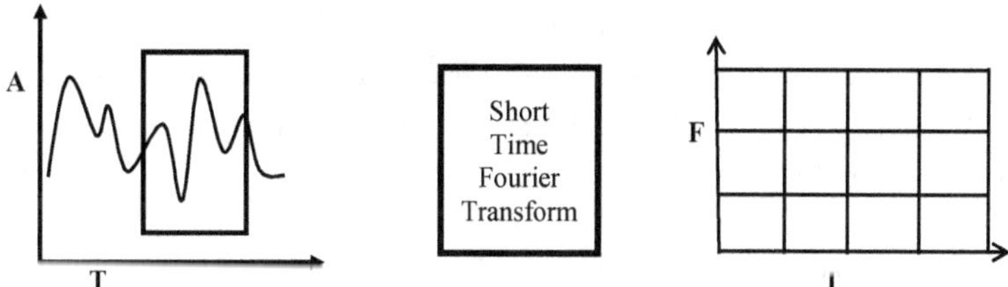

Figure 3.1: Transformation of Signal into STFT

As a conventional transform, the well-known short-time Fourier transform(STFT) is used widely in mathematics and engineering. The STFT represents a sort of compromise between the time and frequency-based views of a signal. It provides some information about both when and at what frequencies a signal event occurs. However, the information of the signal with limited precision can be obtained and that precision is determined by the size of the window.

While the STFT's compromise between time and frequency information can be useful, the drawback is that a particular size for the time window is chosen manually and that window is the same for all frequencies. The STFT employs a sliding window function g(t)that is centered at time t. For each specific τ , a time-localized Fourier transform is performed on the signal x(t) within the window. Subsequently, the window is moved by τ along the time line, and another Fourier transform is performed. Through such consecutive operations, Fourier transform of the entire signal can be performed. The signal segment within the window function is assumed to be approximately stationary. As a result, the STFT decomposes a time domain signal into a 2D time-frequency representation, and variations of the frequency content of that signal within the window function are revealed. The STFT can be expressed as

$$STFT(\tau, f) = \left\langle x, g_{\tau,f} \right\rangle = \int x(t) g_{\tau,f}^{*}(t) = \int x(t) g(t - \tau) e^{-J2\pi ft} dt \quad (3.9)$$

The above equation can also be viewed as a measure of "similarity" between the signal x(t) and the time-shifted and frequency-modulated window function g(t).

3.2.3. *Need for Wavelet Transform in Speech Signal Processing*

A limitation of the STFT is that, because a single window is used for all frequencies, the resolution of the analysis is the same at all locations in the time-frequency plane [Vetterli, 1995]. This limitation represents a handicap in speech and audio signals since human hearing system uses a frequency-dependent resolution. The DWT can solve this drawback with the rectangular tiling of the time frequency plane.

The Wavelet Transform provides a time-frequency representation of the signal. It was developed to overcome the short coming of the Short Time Fourier Transform (STFT), which can also be used to analyze non-stationary signals. While STFT gives a constant resolution at all frequencies, the signals require a more flexible approach to vary the window size to determine more accurately either time or frequency.

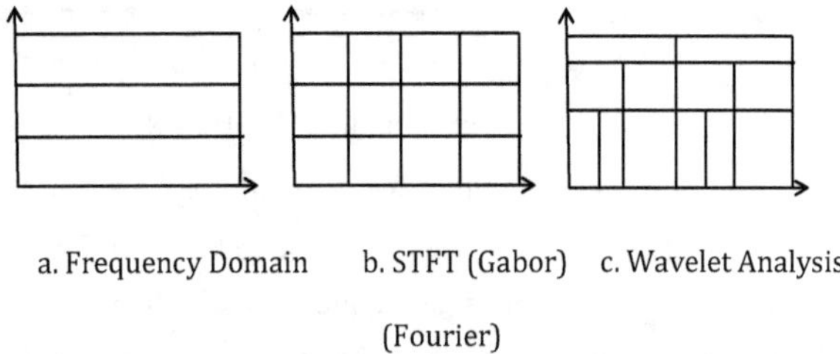

a. Frequency Domain   b. STFT (Gabor)   c. Wavelet Analysis

(Fourier)

Figure 3.2: Fourier, STFT and Wavelet Views of a Signal

The Wavelet Transform uses multi-resolution technique by which different frequencies are analyzed with different resolutions. The wavelet transform enables variable window sizes in analyzing different frequency component switch in a signal [Mallat1999]. This is realized by comparing the signal with a set of template functions obtained from the scaling (i.e., dilation and contraction) and shift (i.e., translation along the time axis) of a base wavelet and looking for their similarities. The wavelet transform of a signal x(t)can be expressed as

$$wt(s,\tau) = \langle x, \psi_{s,\tau} \rangle = \frac{1}{\sqrt{s}} \int_{-\infty}^{\infty} x(t)\psi^* \left(\frac{t-\tau}{s} \right) dt \quad (3.10)$$

where the symbol s > 0 represents the scaling parameter, which determines the time and frequency resolutions of the scaled base wavelet $\psi(t-\tau/s)$. The specific values of s are inversely proportional to the frequency. The symbol τ is the shifting parameter, which translates the scaled wavelet along the time axis. The symbol $\psi^*(t)$ denotes the complex conjugation of the base wavelet $\psi(t)$.

3.2.4. *Comparison of Wavelet Transform with Fourier Transform*

The wavelet transform is often compared with the Fourier transform. Fourier transform (FT) is a powerful tool for analyzing the components of a stationary signal (a stationary signal is a signal where there is no change in the properties of signal). Fourier transform is used to represent a signal as the sum of a series of sines and cosines. While the FT is useful for analysing the spectral content of a stationary signal and it transforms difficult operations into very simple ones in the Fourier dual domain [Cristina Laura Stolojescu, 2008]. But it cannot be used for the analysis of non-stationary signals or for real time applications. The main disadvantage of a Fourier Transform however is that it has only frequency resolution and has no time resolution. This means that although FT can be able to determine all the frequencies present in a signal, it does not know when they are present. To overcome this problem in the past decades several solutions have been developed which are more or less able to represent a signal in the time and frequency domain at the same time.

Wavelet theory extends the ideas of the traditional Fourier theory. The wavelet transform or wavelet analysis is the most recent solution to overcome the shortcomings of the Fourier transform. The Fourier transform is less useful in analyzing non-stationary signal (anon-stationary signal is a signal where there is change in the properties of signal).Wavelet transforms allow the components of a non-stationary signal to be analyzed. Wavelets also allow filters to be constructed for stationary and non-stationary signals [Wells, 1993], [Strang,

1989]. The Fourier transform shows up in a remarkable number of areas outside of classic signal processing. Even taking this into account, we think that it is safe to say that the mathematics of wavelets is much larger than that of the Fourier transform. In fact, the mathematics of wavelets encompasses the Fourier transform. The size of wavelet theory is matched by the size of the application area. Initial wavelet applications involved signal processing and filtering. However, wavelets have been applied in many other areas including non-linear regression and compression. An offshoot of wavelet compression allows the amount of determinism in a time series to be estimated [Wojtaszczyk, 1997].

The main difference is that wavelets are well localized in both time and frequency domain whereas the standard Fourier transform is only localized in frequency domain. The STFT is also time and frequency localized but there are issues with the frequency time resolution and wavelets often give a better signal representation using Multi resolution analysis[Walnut, D.F., 2001].

Why Do We Analyze Wavelet?

All types of signal transmission are based on transmission of a series of numbers. For signal transmission or signal storage the first step is to convert the given information to a series of numbers. To do this we need to represent a function f as a series representation. The function f is stored in the coefficients of the series and we can send only the coefficients. In practice we cannot send an infinite sequence of numbers. It is possible to send only a finite sequence of numbers. For good approximation usually this number forces to be large. For series representation of a function is expressed as

$$f(x) = \sum_{0}^{\infty} a_n f_n(x) \qquad (3.11)$$

Where a_n's are constant coefficients and $f_0, f_1, f_2, \ldots$ are simple functions.

In signal analysis it is common to consider a function in $L_2(R)$.

$$L_2(R) = \left\{ \left\{ f : R \to C \, / \int_R | f(x) |^2 < \infty \right\} \right. \qquad (3.12)$$

This is never periodic except $f = 0$

In that case, wavelet function ψ is expressed as:

$$f(x) = \sum_{j \in Z} \sum_{k \in Z} d_{j,k} \psi_{j,k}(x) \qquad (3.13)$$

where $d_{j,k}$, are wavelet coefficients and $\psi_{j,k}(x) = 2^{j/2} \psi(2^j x - k)$ are the translated and scaled version of wavelet ψ.

For a periodic function the classical method is Fourier transform. But the main drawback of Fourier transform is that we lose our time information which is very important. In the wavelet transform we do not lose the time information, which is useful in many contexts.

3.3.   Fundamentals of Wavelet Theory

Wavelet theory provides a unified framework for a number of techniques that have been developed in various signal processing applications. For example, Multi resolution signal processing, subband coding, speech and image compression. Wavelet theory could naturally play an important role in data mining because wavelets could provide data presentations that enable efficient and accurate mining process and they can also could be incorporated at the kernel for many algorithms [Tao Li, 2005].Wavelet Theory can be used to improve Speech mining performance through two approaches. In the first approach, it can be used as back-end to remove noises. In the second approach, wavelet-based features can be added to other successful features to improve speech processing [M. H. Farouk, 2013]. In this section, bases of wavelet theory are discussed.

What is a Wavelet?

A wave is an oscillating periodic function of time or space. In contrast, wavelets are localized waves. A wavelet is a waveform of limited duration that has an average value of zero. Unlike sinusoids that theoretically extend from minus to plus infinity, wavelets have a beginning and an end. They have their energy concentrated in time or space and are suited to analysis of transient signals. While Fourier transform uses waves to analyze signals, the wavelet transform uses wavelets of finite energy. The plots wave and wavelet are shown in the Figure 3.3.Wavelets are irregular, of limited duration, and often non-symmetrical. They are better at describing anomalies, pulses, and other events that start and stop within the signal.

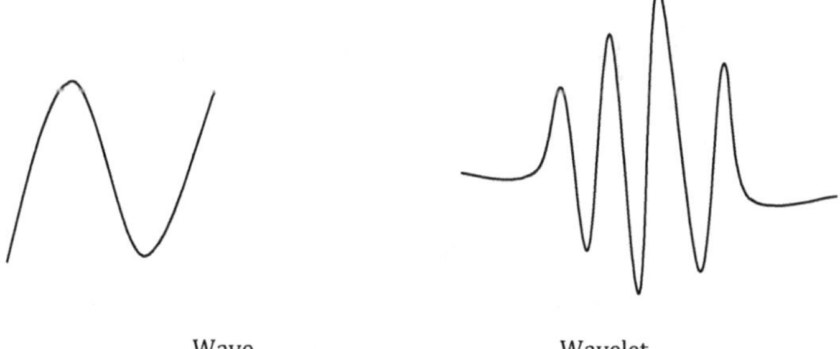

Figure 3.3: Plot of Wave and Wavelet

3.3.1. General Aspects of Wavelets

Wavelets are a recently developed signal processing tool enabling the analysis on several timescales of the local properties of complex signals that can present non-stationary zones. Wavelets are a class of functions to localize a given functions in both position and scaling (Daubechies, 2006). Wavelets are used in application such as signal processing, image processing, time series analysis [Sifuzzaman et al., 2009; Starck et al., 2010; Paris et al, 2011], geophysics, astrophysics, telecommunications, imagery and video coding. They are the foundation for new techniques of signal analysis and synthesis and find beautiful applications to general problems such as compression and denoising. Wavelets form the basis of the wavelet transforms which "cuts up data of functions or operators into different frequency components and then studies each component with a resolution matched to its scale" [Calderbanket al., 1998].

A wavelet transform is a small wave function, usually denoted by $\psi(.)$. A small wave grows and decays in a finite time period, as opposed to a large wave, such as sine wave, which grows and decays repeatedly over an infinite time period. A function ψ (.) which is defined over the real axis $(-\infty, \infty)$ can be classed as a wavelet by satisfying the following three (3) properties:

(1) The integral of $\psi(.)$ is zero:

$$\int_{-\infty}^{\infty} \psi(t)du = 0 \qquad (3.14)$$

(2) The integral of the square of $\psi(.)$ is unity:

$$\int_{-\infty}^{\infty} \psi^2(t)du = 1 \qquad (3.15)$$

(3) Admissibility Condition:

$$C_\psi \equiv \int_0^{\infty} \frac{|\psi(a)|^2}{b} df \text{ Satisfies } 0 < C_\psi < \infty \qquad (3.16)$$

Where t in the above Equations denotes time, a and b denote dilation and translation and C denotes the normalizing factor.

3.3.2. Continuous Wavelet Transformation

The continuous wavelet transform was developed as an alternative approach to the short time Fourier transforms to overcome the resolution problem. The wavelet analysis is done in a similar way to the STFT analysis, in the sense that the signal is multiplied with a function similar to the window function in the STFT, and the transform is computed separately for different segments of the time-domain signal. However, there are two main differences between the STFT and the CWT:

1. The Fourier transforms of the windowed signals are not taken, and therefore single peak will be seen corresponding a sinusoid, i.e., negative frequencies are not computed.

2. The width of the window is changed as the transform is commuted for every single spectral component, which is probably the most significant characteristic of the wavelet transform. The continuous wavelet transform is defined as follows

The term wavelet means a small wave. The smallness refers to the condition that this function is of finite length (compactly supported). The wave refers to the condition that the function is oscillatory. The term mother implies that the functions with different region of support that are used in the transformation process are derived from one main function, or the mother wavelet. In other words, the mother wavelet is a prototype for generating the other window functions.

The continuous wavelet transform is the sum over all time of the signal multiplied by scaled, shifted versions of the wavelet. This process produces wavelet coefficients that are a function of scale and position.CWT of a signal is created with the procedure given in the table 3.1.

Table 3.1: Procedure of Continuous Wavelet Transformation

1.   Take a wavelet and compare it to a section at the start of the original signal.
2.   Calculate a number, C, that represents how closely correlated the wavelet is with the section of the signal. The higher C is, the more the similarity. Note that the results will depend on the shape of the wavelet chosen.
3.   Shift the wavelet to the right and repeat steps 1 and 2 until the whole signal is compared with the wavelet.
4.   Scale (stretch) the wavelet and repeat steps 1 through 3.
5.   Repeat steps 1 through 4 for all scales.

3.3.3. *Discrete Wavelet Transformation*

The discrete wavelet transformation (DWT) scales and positions is based on powers of two (so called *dyadic* scales and positions), the analysis with DWT is much more efficient and accurate. The Discrete Wavelet Transform is obtained by the discretization of the CWT in the time-frequency plane [P. Flandrin, 1993] and is used to decompose discrete time signals. The result obtained at each decomposition level is composed by two types of coefficients: approximation coefficients and detail coefficients. The approximation coefficients are obtained by low-pass filtering the input sequence, followed by down-sampling. The detail coefficients are obtained by high-pass filtering the input sequence followed by down-sampling. The sequence of approximation coefficients constitutes the input for the next iteration. Each decomposition level corresponds to a specified resolution. The resolution decreases with the increasing of the number of decomposition levels. The DWT is invertible. Its inverse is named Inverse DWT (IDWT). At each resolution level, the approximation and the detail sequences are needed for the reconstruction of the approximation signal from the previous resolution level.

The Discrete Wavelet Transform has two features: the wavelet mother and the number of decomposition levels. Discrete wavelets can be scaled and translated in discrete steps and a wavelet representation is the following:

$$\psi_{j,n}(t) = \frac{1}{\sqrt{2^j}} \psi\left(\frac{t - 2^j n}{2^j}\right) \quad (3.17)$$

where j is the scale factor and n is the translation index.

Classical DWT is not shift invariant meaning that the DWT of a translated version of a signal is not the same as the same translation of the DWT of the original signal. In order to achieve shift-invariance, several wavelet transforms have been proposed. The Stationary Wavelet Transform (SWT) overcomes the absence of translation in variance of the DWT. The SWT, also known as the Undecimated Discrete Wavelet Transform (UDWT) is a time-redundant version of the standard DWT [M. J. Shensa, 1992].

Unlike the DWT which down-samples the approximation coefficients and detail coefficients at each decomposition level [Mallat, 1999], SWT does not down-sample. This means that the approximation coefficients and the detail coefficients at each level have the same length as the original signal. This determines an increased number of coefficients at each scale and more accurate localization of signal features. Instead, the filters are up-sampled at each level.

Approximations and Details Coefficients Filtering

For many signals, the low-frequency content is the most important part. It is what gives the signal its identity. The high-frequency content, on the other hand, imparts flavor or nuance. For example, if the high-frequency components are removed from the human voice, the voice sounds are different, but it can still retain what's being said. However, if the low-frequency components are removed, the voice is meaningless. The approximations are the high-scale, low-frequency components of the signal. The details are the low-scale, high-frequency components. The filtering process, at its most basic level is shown in figure 3.4. The original signal, S, passes through two complementary filters and emerges as two signals.

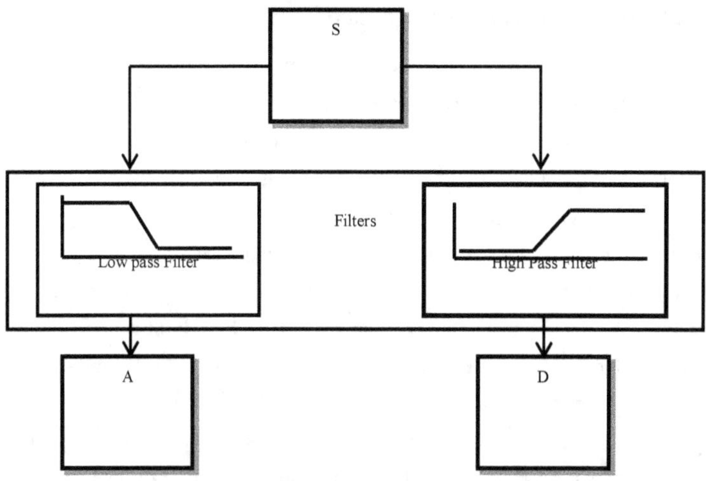

Figure 3.4: Approximation and Detail Components Filtering

Multiple-Level Decomposition

The decomposition process can be iterated, with successive approximations being decomposed in turn, so that one signal is broken down into many lower-resolution components. This is called the **wavelet decomposition tree**. The analysis process is iterative, it can be continued indefinitely. In reality, the decomposition can proceed only until the individual details consist of a single sample or pixel. The decomposition number of levels is based on the nature of the signal, or on a suitable criterion such as entropy.

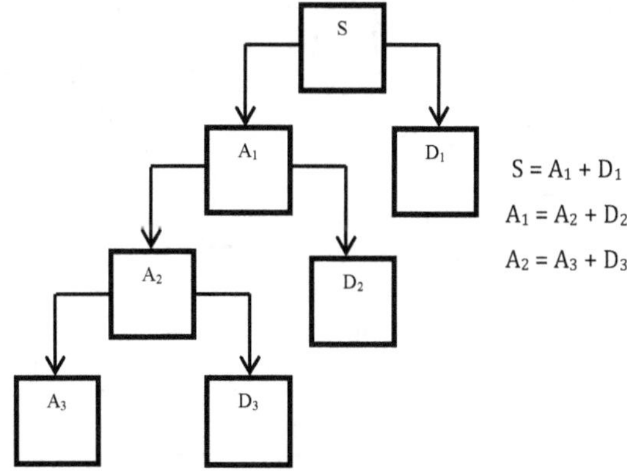

Figure 3.5: Tree level Discrete Wavelet Transformation

3.3.4. *Multi Resolution Analysis of Wavelets*

Although the time and frequency resolution problems are results of a physical phenomenon and exist regardless of the transform used, it is possible to analyze any signal by using an alternative approach called the multi resolution analysis (MRA). MRA, as implied by its name, analyzes the signal at different frequencies with different resolutions. Every spectral component is not resolved equally as was the case in the STFT. MRA is designed to give goodtime resolution and poor frequency resolution at high frequencies and good frequency resolution and poor time resolution at low frequencies. This approach makes sense especially when the signal at hand has high frequency components for short durations and low frequency components for long durations. Fortunately, the signals that are encountered in practical applications are often of this type. Based on the MRA, a signal is decomposed into an approximation and details at various scales. In other words, various information levels across successive resolutions can be extracted by decomposing the original signal using a wavelet ortho normal basis.

3.3.5. *Wavelet Packet Analysis*

The wavelet packet method is a generalization of wavelet decomposition that offers a richer range of possibilities for signal analysis. In wavelet analysis, a signal is split into an approximation and a detail. The approximation is then itself split into a second-level approximation and detail, and the process is repeated. For a n-level decomposition, there are n+1possible ways to decompose or encode the signal.

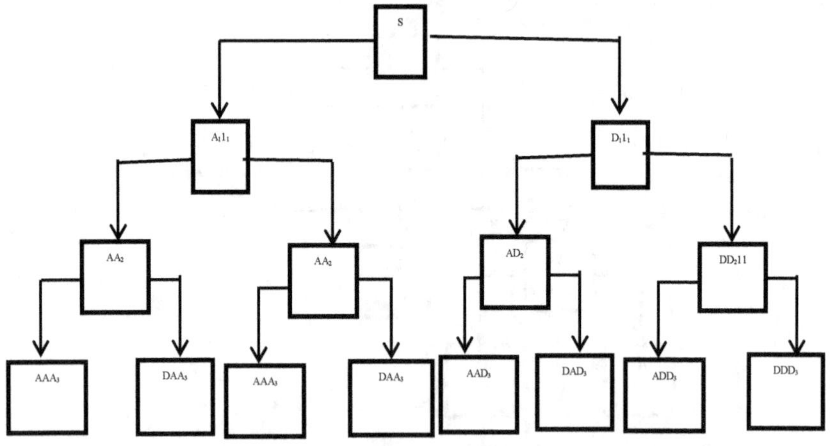

Figure 3.6: Three level Decomposition of Wavelet Packet

In wavelet packet analysis, the details as well as the approximations can be split. This yields 2n different ways to encode the signal. This is the wavelet packet decomposition tree.

For instance, wavelet packet analysis allows the signal S to be represented as:

$$S = A1 + AAD3 + DAD3 + DD2$$

This is an example of a representation that is not possible with ordinary wavelet analysis.

3.4. Functioning of Wavelet Theory as Data Mining Tool

Wavelet theory could naturally play an important role in data mining since it is well founded and of very practical use. Wavelets have many favorable properties, such as vanishing moments, hierarchical and multi resolution decomposition structure, linear time and space complexity of the transformations, decorrelated coefficients, and a wide variety of basic functions. These properties could provide considerably more efficient and effective solutions to many data mining problems. First, wavelets could provide presentations of data that make the mining process more efficient and accurate. Second, wavelets could be incorporated into the kernel of many data mining algorithms. Although standard wavelet applications are mainly on data which have temporal or spatial localities (e.g. time series, stream data, and image data) wavelets have also been successfully applied to diverse domains in data mining. In practice, a wide variety of wavelet-related methods have been applied to a wide range of data mining problems.

3.5. Some Applications of Wavelets

Wavelets are a powerful statistical tool which can be used for a wide range of applications, namely

- Signal processing
- Data compression
- Smoothing and image denoising
- Fingerprint verification
- Biology for cell membrane recognition, to distinguish the normal from the
- pathological membranes
- DNA analysis, protein analysis
- Blood-pressure, heart-rate and ECG analyses
- Finance (which is more surprising), for detecting the properties of quick
- variation of values
- In Internet traffic description, for designing the services size

- Industrial supervision of gear-wheel

- Speech recognition

- Computer graphics and multi-fractal analysis

- Many areas of physics have seen this paradigm shift, including molecular dynamics, astrophysics, optics, turbulence and quantum mechanics.

3.6.   Some Advantages of Wavelet Theory

- One of the main advantages of wavelets is that they offer a simultaneous localization in time and frequency domain.

- The second main advantage of wavelets is that, using fast wavelet transform, it is computationally very fast.

- Wavelets have the great advantage of being able to separate the fine details in a signal. Very small wavelets can be used to isolate very fine details in a signal, while very large wavelets can identify coarse details.

- A wavelet transform can be used to decompose a signal into component wavelets.

- In wavelet theory, it is often possible to obtain a good approximation of the given function f by using only a few coefficients which is the great achievement in compare to Fourier transform.

- Most of the wavelet coefficients $\left\{ dj.k \right\}_{|j|,|k|>=N}$ vanish for large N.

- Wavelet theory is capable of revealing aspects of data that other signal analysis techniques miss the aspects like trends, breakdown points, and discontinuities in higher derivatives and self-similarity.

3.7.   Wavelet Families

Wavelets are mathematical functions that cut up data into different frequency components, and then study each component with a resolution matched to its scale. They have advantages over traditional Fourier methods in analyzing physical situations where the signal contains discontinuities and sharp spikes. Wavelet families vary in terms of several important properties. The properties are:

- Support of the wavelet in time and frequency and rate of decay.

- Symmetry or anti-symmetry of the wavelet. The accompanying perfect reconstruction filters have linear phase.

- Number of vanishing moments. Wavelets with increasing numbers of vanishing moments result in sparse representations for a large class of signals and images.

- Regularity of the wavelet. Smoother wavelets provide sharper frequency resolution. Additionally, iterative algorithms for wavelet construction converge faster.
- Existence of a scaling function, φ.

Table 3.2: List of Wavelets and their Family Names

Wavelet Name	Wavelet Family Name
haar	Haar wavelet
db	Daubechies wavelets
sym	Symlets
coif	Coiflets
bior	Biorthogonal wavelets
meyr	Meyer wavelet
morl	Morlet wavelet

3.7.1. Haar Wavelet

Haar, the first and simplest. Haar is discontinuous, and resembles a step function. It represents the same wavelet as Daubechies db1.The Haar wavelet is a sequence of rescaled, square-shaped functions which together form a wavelet family or basis. The wavelet is the simplest type of wavelet. In discrete form, Haar wavelets are related to a mathematical operation called the Haar transform (HT). The Haar transform decomposes a discrete signal into two sub signals of half its length. A HT decomposes each signal into two components, one is called average (approximation) and the other is known as difference (detail) [S.S. Tamboli1, 2013], [Kannan, 2010]. [Kannan, 2010]. The technical disadvantage of the Haar wavelet is that it is not continuous. This property can, however, be useful for the analysis of signals with sudden transitions, such as monitoring of tool failures in machines.

3.7.2. Daubechies Wavelet

The dbN wavelets are the Daubechies' extremal phase wavelets. N refers to the number of vanishing moments. The db1 wavelet is the same as Haar. Daubechies wavelet family is the most widely used orthogonal wavelet family and is named in the honour of its inventor, the Belgian physicist and mathematician Ingrid Daubechies. They represent a collection of orthogonal mother wavelets with compact support, characterized by a maximal number of vanishing moments for some given length of the support. Corresponding to each mother wavelets from this class, there is a scaling function(also called father wavelet) which generates an orthogonal MRA. The Daubechies wavelet transforms are defined in the same way as the Haar wavelet transform by computing the running averages and differences via scalar products with scaling signals and wavelets the only difference between them consists in how these scaling signals and wavelets are defined. The Daubechies wavelet is more complicated than the Haar wavelet. DbN wavelets provide us with a set of powerful tools for performing basic speech processing tasks. These tasks include compression and noise removal for audio signals and speech recognition.

3.7.3. Symlet Wavelet

Symlets (symN, where N is the order), also known as Daubechies least asymmetric mother wavelets. They are compact supported, orthogonal, continuous, but only nearly symmetric mother wavelets. The purpose was to create wavelets with the same size and same number of vanishing moments as Daubechies, but with near linear phase filters. Symlets have the highest number of vanishing moments for a given support width. Symlets have N/2 vanishing moments, support length N-1 and filter length N. The properties of the two wavelet families are similar. There are 7 different Symlets functions from sym2 to sym8.

3.7.4. Coiflets Wavelet

Coiflets (coifN, where N is the order) are discrete wavelets designed by Ingrid Daubechies and named in the honor of Ronald Coifman who was another researcher in the field of wavelets theory. Coiflets are compactly supported wavelets and were designed to be more symmetrical than Daubechies mother wavelets to have a support of size N-1 and filter length N. The number next to the wavelet's name represents the number of vanishing moments, related to the number of wavelet coefficients.

3.7.5. Bi orthogonal Wavelet

This family of wavelets exhibits the property of linear phase, which is needed for signal and image reconstruction. By using two wavelets, one for decomposition and the other for reconstruction instead of the same single one, interesting properties are derived.

3.7.6. Meyer Wavelet

The Meyer wavelet and scaling function are defined in the frequency domain. The Meyer wavelet is an orthogonal wavelet proposed by Yves Meyer. As a type of a continuous wavelet, it has been applied in a number of cases, such as in adaptive filters, fractal random fields and multi-fault classification.

3.7.7. Morlet Wavelet

The Morlet wavelet (or Gabor wavelet) is a wavelet composed of a complex exponential multiplied by a Gaussian window. This wavelet is closely related to human perception, both hearing and vision.

The Properties of Wavelets

The properties of wavelets are given below and are listed in the table 3.3.

- Computation Complexity
- Vanishing Moments
- Compact Support
- Decorrelated Coefficients
- Parseval's Theorem:

Table 3.3: Summary of Wavelet Families and Associated Properties [Chui C. K., 1992]

	morl	mexh	meyr	haar	dbN	symN	coifN	biorNr.Nd
"Crude"	✓	✓						
Infinitely regular	✓	✓	✓					
Compactly supported Orthogonal				✓	✓	✓	✓	
Compactly supported Biothogonal								✓
Symmetry	✓	✓	✓	✓				✓
Asymmetry					✓			
Near symmetry						✓	✓	
Arbitrary number of vanishing moments					✓	✓	✓	✓
Vanishing moments for Φ							✓	
Arbitrary regularity					✓	✓	✓	✓
Existence of Φ			✓	✓	✓	✓	✓	✓
Orthogonal analysis			✓	✓	✓	✓	✓	
Biorthogonal analysis			✓	✓	✓	✓	✓	✓
Exact reconstruction			✓	✓	✓	✓	✓	✓
FIR filters			✓	✓	✓	✓	✓	✓
Continuous transform				✓	✓	✓	✓	✓
Discrete transform	✓	✓	✓	✓	✓	✓	✓	✓
Fast algorithm			✓	✓	✓	✓	✓	✓
Explicit expression	✓	✓		✓		✓	✓	for splines

3.8. Discussion

The wavelet transform is a revolution of modern signal processing techniques and most widely used for various signal related applications. The Wavelet Transform provides a time-frequency representation of the signal. Significant contributions of wavelet analysis to different signal processing techniques have been developed for signal, and speech processing applications. The Fourier transform is the most widely applied signal processing tool in signal processing. But it cannot be used for the analysis of non-stationary signals or for real time applications. The wavelet transform or wavelet analysis is the most recent solution to overcome the shortcomings of the Fourier transform. Various speech transformation techniques, wavelets and their properties are discussed.

CHAPTER 4

FEATURE EXTRACTION TECHNIQUES OF SPEECH

4.1. Introduction

Feature extraction is the most important phase in speech processing system. Features are extracted from the speech signals on the basis of short term amplitude spectrum.It is the mathematic representation of the speech file.The features carry the characteristics of the useful information regarding speech. In the context of Automatic Speech Recognition (ASR) feature extraction is the process of retaining the useful information from the speech signal while the unnecessary and unwanted information is removed. The extracted features are involved in further speech signal analysis. However, while removing the unwanted information from the speech signal some useful information may be lost. The main objective of feature extraction is to untangle the speech signal into the different acoustically identifiable components and to obtain the set of feature with low rate of change in order to keep the computation feasible.

The goal of feature extraction is to compute saving sequence of feature vectors for providing compact representation of input signal. Feature extraction is performed in three stages. First stage (feature generation) is speech analysis or acoustic front end. This step performs spectra temporal analysis of signal. The second stage (feature representation) compiles extended feature vector composed of static and dynamic features. The third stage (dimensionality reduction) transforms the extended feature vectors into more compact and robust vectors which are to be applied to the classification. The basic steps of feature extraction process are shown in the following figure 4.1.

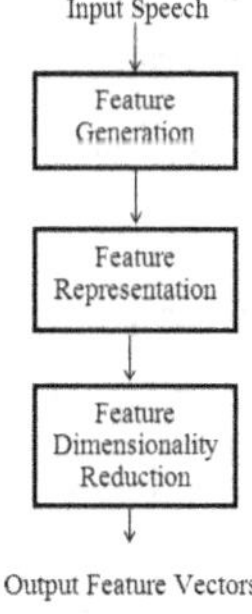

Figure 4.1: Various Stages of Feature Extraction Process

4.2. Fundamental Frequency of Signal

A speech signal consists of different frequencies which are harmoniously related to each other in the form of a series. The lowest frequency of this harmonious series is known as the fundamental frequency or pitch frequency.

Pitch frequency is the fundamental frequency of the vocal cords. Many different techniques available to find the fundamental frequency (f0) like auto correlation method and FFT based extraction method.

The following steps are followed to extract fundamental frequency.

1. Take the spoken word or utterance
2. Take FFT of the above signal with certain point number.
3. Track the first peak in the FFT output to find the fundamental frequency. Frequency resolution is decided by FFT point number
4. Multiply the FFT point number by frequency resolution to obtain the fundamental frequency.

4.3. Feature Extraction Techniques

In speech recognition, the main goal of the feature extraction step is to compute a sequence of feature vectors providing a compact representation of the given input signal. Commonly LPC, MFCC, PLP, LDA and PCA are used as feature extraction techniques for speech processing system.

4.3.1. *Linear Predictive Coding (LPC)*

In the area of speech processing, the Linear Predictive Coding (LPC) is oneof the robust and dynamic speech analysis techniques. It is also powerful forspeech encoding using the lowest bit rate. This technique provides basicspeech parameter and which can be used for efficient computation of performance evaluation. The variation of LPC depends on intensity, frequency, pitch and formant. The number of LPC coefficient is executedfrom run source through filter on resulted coefficient of speech.

LPC feature extraction process can be explained from following figure 4.2.

The input speech signal digitized spectrally flatten speech signal is put through a low order digital system to make it less susceptible to finite precision effects later in the signal processing.

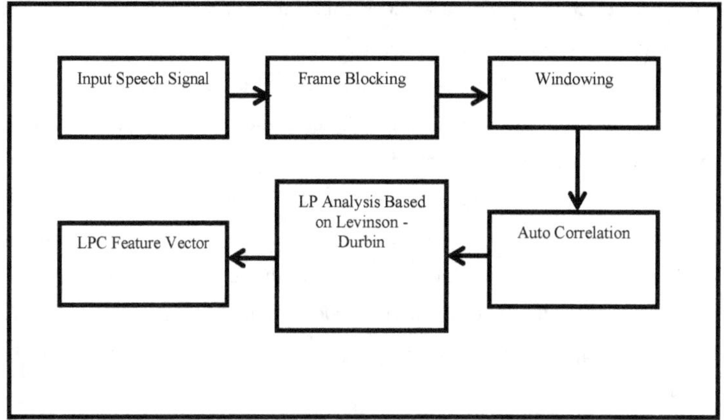

Figure 4.2: Block Diagram of LPC Feature Extraction Technique

To compute LPC features, initially the speech signal is blocked into frames of N samples. After frame blocking, the next step is to window each individual frame so as to minimize the signal discontinuities at the beginning and end of each frame. Typical window is the Hamming window.The next step is to auto correlate each frame of windowed signal Where the highest autocorrelation value is the order of the LPC analysis. The next processing step is the LPC analysis, which converts each frame of autocorrelations into LPC parameter set by using Durbin's method. LPC cepstral coefficients, is a very important LPC parameter set, which can be derived directly from the LPC coefficient set.

4.3.2. *Mel- Frequency Cepstrum Coefficient (MFCC)*

MFCC is one of the most popular feature extraction techniques used in speech recognition. It is based on the frequency domain of Mel scale for human ear scale. Speech signal had been expressed in the Mel frequency scale, in order to capture the important characteristics of speech.

Bassam et al. [B. Al-Qatab and R.Ainon, 2010] developed and implemented an Arabic speech recognition system using Hidden Markov Model Toolkit and used MFCC for feature extraction. In [Y. Alotaibi, M. Alghamdi and F. Alotaiby, 2008] the authors designed an isolated word recognizer with phoneme based HMM models and MFCC features. MFCC feature extraction is one of the more popular parameterization methods used by researchers in the speech technology field. It has the benefit that it is capable of capturing the phonetically important characteristics of speech. It gives a good discrimination and a small correlation between components.

The set of coefficients computed in MFCC is called acoustic vectors. Therefore, each input utterance is transformed into a sequence of acoustic vectors. A block diagram of the MFCC processes is shown in Figure 4.3. Block diagram of MFCC The speech waveform is cropped to remove silence or acoustical interference that may be present in the beginning or end of the sound file. The windowing block minimizes the discontinuities of the signal by tapering the beginning and end of each frame to zero. The FFT block converts each frame from the time domain to the frequency domain. In the Mel-frequency wrapping block, the signal is plotted against the Mel spectrum to mimic human hearing. In the final step, the Cepstrum, the Mel spectrum scale is converted back to standard frequency scale. This spectrum provides a good representation of the spectral properties of the signal which is the key for representing and recognizing characteristics of the speaker.

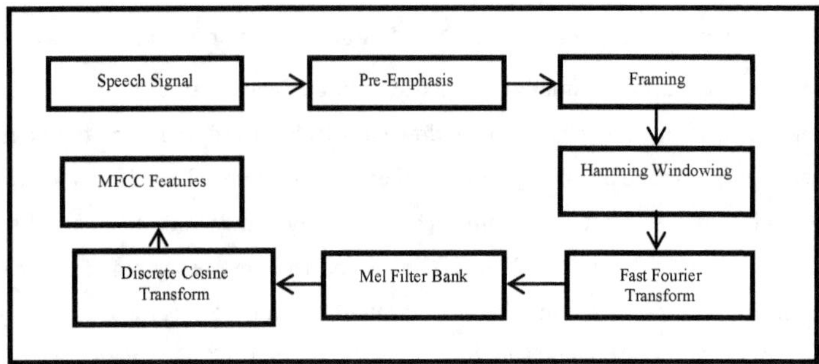

Figure 4.3: Block Diagram of MFCC Feature Extraction Technique

Table 4.1: Computing Steps in MFCC Feature Extraction Process

Step1	Speech is first divided into short frames over the range it can be considered quasi-stationary.
Step2	Fourier transform of each frame of the signal is obtained.
Step3	Mel scaling is applied using triangular overlapping windows. There are many variationsin the number of and kind of filter bank used.
Step4	Take the log of the power at each of the mel frequencies.
Step5	Take the discrete cosine transform (DCT) of the mel log power. These mel-scaled scaled cepstrum exist in a domain referred as frequency which has the same unit as time.
Step6	The MFCCs are the amplitudes of the resulting spectrum.

4.3.3. Linear Discriminant Analysis

Linear Discriminant Analysis (LDA) is commonly used technique for dataclassification and dimensionality reduction. It easily handles the case where within-class frequencies are unequal and their performances have beenexamined on randomly generated test data. This method maximizes the ratioof between-class variance to the within class variance in any particular data set thereby guaranteeing maximal reparability. The use of Linear Discriminant Analysis for data classification is applied to classification problem of speech recognition [Kashyap Patel, R. K. and Prasad, 2013]. LDA algorithm provides betterclassification compared to principal components analysis [Oh-Wook et al, 2003].

4.3.4. Principal Component Analysis (PCA)

PCA is a well-established technique for feature extraction and dimensionality reduction. It is based on the assumption that most information about classes is contained in the directions along where the variations are the large. The most common derivation of PCA is in terms of a standardized linear projection which maximizes the variance in the projected space. Principal components analysis (PCA) is a method of identifying patterns in data, and highlights their similarities and differences. It is powerful tool for analyzing data. The main advantage of PCA is that once the patterns in the data are found then compression may be done i.e. dimension may be reduced.

4.3.5. Perceptual linear Prediction (PLP)

The Perceptual Linear Prediction model developed by Hermansky discards irrelevant information of speech and thus improves speech recognition rate. PLP is similar to LPC analysis, which is based on the short-term spectrum of speech. In contrast to pure linear predictive analysis of speech, perceptual linear prediction (PLP) modifies the short-term spectrum of the speech. PLP technique is an auditory-like spectrum based on linear predictive analysis of speech. PLP combines several engineering approximations in modeling the psychophysical attributes of human hearing such as the critical band (Bark) frequency resolution, asymmetries of auditory filters, unequal sensitivity of human hearing at different frequencies, intensity-loudness non-linear relationship and broader than critical-band integration [A. M. Toh, 2007].

Park et al. [2009] explored the training and adaptation of multilayer perceptron (MLP) features in Arabic ASRs. Three schemes had been investigated. First, the use of MLP features to incorporate short-vowel information into the grapheme system. Second, a rapid training approach for use with the PLP + MLP system is described. Finally, the use of linear input networks (LIN) adaptation as an alternative to the usual HMM-based linear adaptation was demonstrated. PLP is affected by factors such as the recording equipment, the communication channel or additive noise. It is an all-pole model, like LPC, so its advantages and disadvantages are similar to those of LPC but PLP is more complex and computationally intensive.

4.3.6. Rasta-PLP

RASTA is short for RelAtive SpecTrAl. It is a technique which is used to enhance the speech when recorded in a noisy environment. The Perceptual linear prediction analysis depends on short term spectrum of the speech. For the improvement of a result in PLP the short term spectrum of the speech by different psychologically based transformation is used. The Linear Predictive speech analysis technique is based on short term spectrum of speech. It is one of the most powerful speech analysis technique and most useful methods for encoding good quality speech at a low bit rate. It provides extremely accurate estimation of speech parameters. The short-term spectral values are modified by the frequency response of communication, which makes this technique vulnerable. Rasta processing is an approach of feature extraction, enhancement and suppression for speech recognition. Rasta processing increases dependence of the data on its previous context. The Rasta processing works well in word model. The RASTA filter can be used either in the log spectral or Cepstral domains.

4.3.7. Phonetic Posteriorgram Representation

A phonetic posteriorgram is defined by a probability vector representing the posterior probabilities of a set of pre-defined phonetic classes for a speech frame. By using an independently trained phonetic recognizer, each input speech frame can be converted to its corresponding posteriorgram representation. Given a spoken sample of a keyword, the frames belonging to the keyword are converted to a series of phonetic posteriorgrams by a full phonetic recognition [Hazen, 2009]. Then, they use dynamic time warping to calculate the distortion scores between the keyword posteriorgrams and the posteriorgrams of the test utterances.

The detection result is given by ranking the distortion scores. The most recent work by Hazen et al. [2009] showed a spoken keyword detection system using phonetic posteriorgram templates.

4.3.8. Gaussian Posteriorgram Representation

A Gaussian posteriorgram is defined as a probability vector representing the posterior probabilities of a set of Gaussian components for a speech frame. The generation of a Gaussian posteriorgram is divided into two phases. In the first phase, a Gaussian mixture Model (GMM) is trained on all the training data and this GMM is used to produce a raw Gaussian posteriorgram vector for each speech frame. In the second phase, a discounting based smoothing technique is applied to each posteriorgram vector.

Table 4.2: The Feature Extraction Technique with their Comparative Properties [Anusuya M.A and Katti S.K., 2009]

Feature Extraction Techniques	Properties
Mel-Frequency Cestrum Coefficient (MFFCs)	• Power spectrum is computed by • performing Fourier Analysis, • Robust and dynamic method for • speech feature extraction
Principal Component analysis (PCA)	• Eigenvector-based method. • Nonlinear feature extraction method • Supported to Linear map. • Faster than other technique. • It is good for Gaussian data.
Linear Discriminate Analysis(LDA)	• Linear feature extraction method • Supported to supervised linear map. • Faster than other technique, • Better than PCA for classification.
Linear Predictive coding	• Static feature extraction Method. • It is used for feature Extraction at • lower order coefficient.
Wavelet Technique	• Better time resolution than Fourier • Transform, Real time factor is • minimum

4.4. Statistical Features Extraction

Mean

An Arithmetic Mean is mathematical representation of the typical value of a set of data, computed as the sum of all the numbers in the dataset divided by the size of the dataset. Suppose there is sample space $\{x_1, x_2, x_3....x_n\}$ then the arithmetic mean μ_x is defined as the means of the raw signals:

$$\mu_x = \frac{1}{N} \sum_{N}^{1} X_n \quad (4.1)$$

Standard Deviation

Standard deviation shows how much variation or dispersion exists from the mean. A low standard deviation indicates that the data points tend to be very close to the mean, whereas the high standard deviation indicates that the data points are spread out over a large range of values. Let X is a random variable with mean value μ. Here the operator E denotes the average or expected value of X. Then the standard deviation of X is:

$$\sigma_x = \left[\frac{1}{N-1}\right]\sum_{n=1}^{N}(X_n - \mu_x) \qquad (4.2)$$

Variance

Basically variance is a statistical parameter which gives information about data distribution from its mean or expected value. It is the one type of probability distribution whichmeasures how far a set of numbers get spread. The variance is calculated as:

$$\sigma_i^2 = \sum_{i=0}^{N-1}\sum_{j=0}^{N-1} P_{i,j}(i-\mu_i)^2 \qquad (4.3)$$

$$\sigma_j^2 = \sum_{j=0}^{N-1}\sum_{j=0}^{N-1} P_{i,j}(i-\mu_j)^2 \qquad (4.4)$$

Skewness

Skewness is the third moment of the data distribution. It measures the symmetry of the data. If data distribution seems to be similar the same to the left and right of the center point it shows symmetric property and always symmetric data has skewness near zero whereas skewness for normal distribution is zero. Negative value of skewness shows data that are skewed left and positive values of the skewness shows data that are skewed right. Skewness is represented by the formula:

$$s = \sum_{j=0}^{N-1}(i-\mu)^3 P(i) \qquad (4.5)$$

Entropy

Entropy is a numerical measure of the randomness of a signal. Entropy can act as a feature and is used to analyzetime series data such as speech signal. The Entropy is the statistical descriptor of the variability within the speech signal and is a strong feature for emotion classification.

It can be mathematically represented as

$$e = -\sum_{1}^{n} x^2 - \log(x^2) \qquad (4.6)$$

The simplest and the most common approach use histogram-based estimation, but other approaches have been developed and used, each with its own benefits and drawbacks. The main factor in choosing a method is often a trade-off between the bias and the variance of the estimate although the nature of the (suspected) distribution of the data may also be a factor.

In various science or engineering applications, such as independent component analysis, image analysis, genetic analysis, speech recognition, manifold learning, and time delay estimation it is useful to estimate the differential entropy of a system or process when given some observations.

Power

Power is Measure of the amplitude of speech signal and the power can be calculated as:

$$Power = \sum \frac{X^2}{L(X)} \qquad (4.7)$$

Where, X = is the signal values and L(x) = Length of the signal.

Power is also defined as the amount of energy consumed per unit time. The unit of power is the joule per second (J/s), known as the watt. Energy transfer can be used to do work, so power is the rate at which this work is performed.

Root Mean Square (RMS) Value

The RMS value of a set of values is the square root of the arithmetic mean (average) of the squares of the original values (or the square of the function that defines the continuous waveform). In the case of a set of n values $\{x_1, x_2, x_3 .... x_n\}$, the RMS value is given by the formula:

$$X_{rms} = \sqrt{b^2 \frac{1}{n}(X_1^2 + X_2^2 + ... + X_n^2)} \qquad (4.8)$$

In mathematics, the RMS, also known as the quadratic mean, is a statistical measure of the magnitude of a varying quantity. It is especially useful when varieties are positive and negative, e.g., sinusoids. RMS is used in various fields, including speech processing, image processing and electrical engineering. It can be calculated for a series of discrete values or for a continuously varying function. Its name comes from its definition as the square root of the mean of the squares of the values.

Smoothness

Smoothness is a measure of the rhythmic pattern of acceleration and deceleration of signal. The measure of smoothness is calculated as:

$$R = 1 - \frac{1}{1 + \sigma^2} \qquad (4.9)$$

Where the bounded measure $0 <= \sigma^2 <= 1$.

4.5.   Discussion

Feature vector is the mathematic representation of the speech. Various feature extraction techniques which are used to represent speech signals are presented. The features carry the characteristics of the useful information regarding speech. The speech signal consists of different frequencies. The lowest frequency is known as the fundamental frequency of the signal. Fundamental frequency extraction technique is discussed. Various Feature extraction techniques are discussed in brief. The MFCC feature extraction is one of the most widely used techniques with stationary speech signals. Also selected statistical feature extraction parameters are discussed in this chapter.

CHAPTER 5

WAVELET PACKET TRANSFORMATION BASED MODEL FOR KEYWORD SPOTTING

5.1. Introduction

Keyword spotting in continuous speech is considered as a challenging issue due to dynamic nature of speech. To identify the keyword from speech signals and reveal the underlying dynamics that corresponds to the speech signals, proper signal processing technique is needed. Typically, the process of signal processing transforms a time-domain signal into another domain, with the purpose of extracting the characteristic information embedded within the signal that is otherwise not readily observable in its original form.

Wavelet theory has become one of the most important and powerful tool of signal representation [Bahi,2009]. Wavelet transforms are suitable tools for analyzing non-stationary signals. Since speech consists of both high and low frequency components, short and long duration sounds, the wavelet transform is well suited to this type of analysis. In many speech related applications, wavelets are used to perform preprocessing (e.g. noise filtering), dimensionality reduction and data transformation.

Fourier transform theory states that a given function of time can be characterized either in time or in frequency (spectral) domain. The transformation of a signal $x(t)$ between the time domain and the frequency domain can be done by computing the Fourier transform. Fourier transform is indispensable as data analysis tool for stationary signals. But if we deal with non-stationary signals the conventional Fourier transform becomes inadequate. Time-frequency (time-scale) representation techniques overcome this problem as they are capable of representing a given function of time in both time and frequency domain simultaneously.

Wavelets are mathematical functions that cut up data into different frequency components, and then study each component with a resolution matched to its scale. They have advantages over traditional Fourier methods in analyzing physical situations where the signal contains discontinuities and sharp spikes. Wavelet algorithms process data at different scales or resolutions. Wavelets are well-suited for approximating data with sharp discontinuities. The wavelet analysis procedure is to adopt a wavelet prototype.

The time resolution and frequency resolution of a STFT basis element is equal to those of the window. Narrow windows give good time resolution, but poor frequency resolution. Wide windows give good frequency resolution, but poor time resolution and may also violate the condition of stationary, for signals which are stationary on portions. The effect of the selection of a window too long will be the smoothening of the analyzed signal and the information contained in its parts with rapid variations will be recovered with difficulty from its STFT. So, the window should be carefully chosen because it does not change during the period of analysis. Therefore, the time and frequency resolutions will remain unchanged on the entire duration of the analysis performed using the STFT, these resolutions being imposed by the window selected.

Wavelets are a recently developed signal processing tool enabling the analysis on several timescales of the local properties of complex signals that can present non-stationary zones. The Continuous Wavelet Transform (CWT) was an alternative approach to the STFT, to overcome the problem of constant resolution. It is done in a similar way as the STFT, in the sense that the signal is multiplied with a function, the wavelet, similar to the window function in the STFT. The transform is computed separately for different segments of the time-domain. This transform is capable of providing the time and frequency information simultaneously, hence giving a time-frequency representation of the signal.

A wavelet is used to analyze a given function or continuous-time signal at a specified scale. This function plays the role of the window from the case of STFT, but it has a second parameter, additional to the position, the scale. It can be moved to various locations of the signal as shown in Figure 5.1.

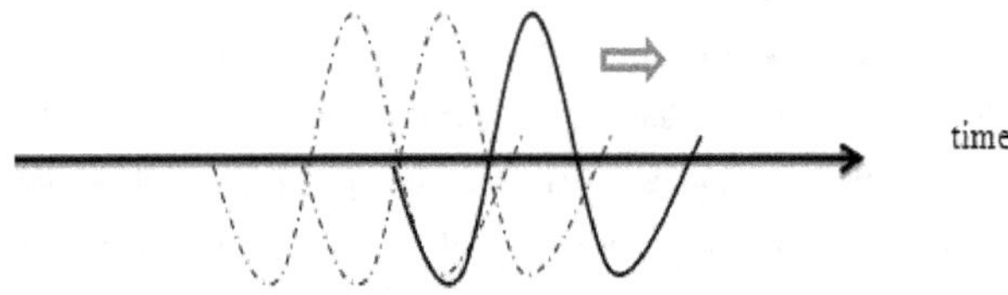

Figure 5.1: Location in Time of a Wavelet with a Given Scale

To analyze signal structures of very different sizes, it is necessary to use time-frequency atoms with different time supports. A linear time-frequency transform correlates the signal with a family of waveforms that are well concentrated in time and in frequency. These wave forms are called time-frequency atoms [P. Flandrin, 1993].

Hence, wavelet transformation of speech signal is needed and is to be applied to develop an approach for keyword spotting system. This chapter proposes an algorithm for keyword spotting using wavelet packet decomposition with sliding window frames.

5.2. Time-frequency Representations

Fourier transform theory states that a given function of time can be characterized either in time or in frequency (spectral) domain. The transformation of a signal x(t) between the time domain and the frequency domain can be done by computing the Fourier transform. Fourier transform is indispensable as data analysis tool for stationary signals. But if we deal with non-stationary signals the conventional Fourier transform becomes in adequate. Time-frequency (time-scale) representation techniques overcome this problem as they are capable of representing a given function of time in both time and frequency domain simultaneously. These kinds of representations aim to identify the parameters of a given signal: the starting/ending moments, the energy or the power, the instantaneous amplitude, the instantaneous frequency, the instantaneous frequency band, etc. [A. Isar and I. Nafornita, 1998].

5.3. Wavelet Transformation of Speech

Wavelet transforms are suitable tools for analyzing non-stationary signals. Since speech consists of both high and low frequency components, short and long duration sounds, the wavelet transform is well suited to this type of analysis. In many speech related applications, wavelets are used to perform preprocessing (e.g. noise filtering), dimensionality reduction and data transformation. Wavelet theory provides a unified framework for a number of techniques that have been developed in various signal processing applications. For example, Multi resolution signals processing, subband coding, speech and image compression. Wavelet Theory can be used to improve Speech processing performance through two approaches. In the first approach, it can be used as back-end to remove noises. In the second approach, wavelet-based features can be added to other successful features to improve speech processing [Davis, 1980]. In this section, bases of wavelet theory are discussed. The two most commonly used forms of the wavelet transforms are the continuous wavelet transform and the discrete wavelet transform.

5.3.1. Continuous Wavelet Transform

A continuous wavelet transform (CWT) is used to divide a continuous-time function into wavelets. Unlike Fourier transform, the continuous wavelet transform possesses the ability to construct a time-frequency representation of a signal that offers very good time and frequency localization. The CWT is similar to the Fourier transform where an arbitrary function of time can be represented by an infinite summation of sinusoidal functions and their multiplicative coefficients. In wavelet analysis sinusoidal functions are replaced with wavelet functions. The essence of the calculation is then to determine the coefficients necessary to accurately portray the time function.

In definition, the continuous wavelet transform is a convolution of the input data sequence with a set of functions generated by the mother wavelet. The convolution can be computed by using a Fast Fourier Transform (FFT) algorithm. Normally, the output is a real valued function except when the mother wavelet is complex. A complex mother wavelet will convert the continuous wavelet transform to a complex valued function.

The CWT compares the signal to shifted and compressed or stretched versions of a wavelet. Stretching or compressing a function is collectively referred to as *dilation* or *scaling* and corresponds to the physical notion of *scale*. By comparing the signal to the wavelet at various scales and positions, a function of two variables is obtained.

5.3.2. *Discrete Wavelet Transform*

The CWT is a computationally demanding algorithm so, as with Fourier techniques, the discrete wavelet transform has been developed. The DWT differs from the CWT in that the method of computation utilizes sub-band coding. As there is a great deal of redundancy in the data contained within the CWT, the DWT utilizes sampling of both scale and time data, thereby producing a substantially faster algorithm.

The Discrete Wavelet Transform provides a compact representation of a signal in time and frequency that can be computed efficiently [George Tzanetakis, 2000]. For many signals, the low-frequency part contains the most important part. It gives an identity to a signal. In wavelet analysis, the speech signal is split into approximations and details components. The approximations are the high scale, low frequency components of the signal. The details are the low-scale, high frequency components. Filters are one of the most widely used signal processing functions. Wavelets can be realized by iteration of filters with rescaling. The filtering operation is used to determine the resolution of the signal, which is a measure of the amount of detail information in the signal and the scale is determined by up sampling and down sampling operations[Vimal Krishnan, et al, 2009]. The DWT is computed by successive low pass and high pass filtering of the discrete time-domain signal as shown in Fig. 5.2 and Fig. 5.3.

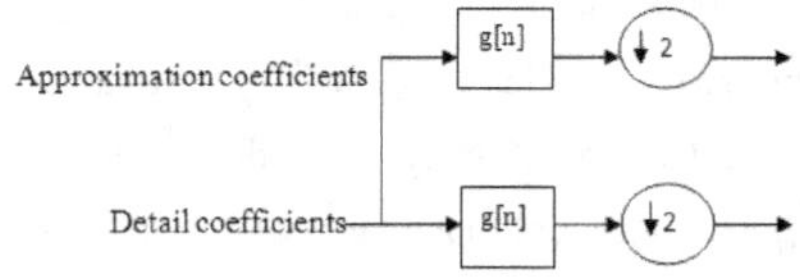

Figure 5.2: DWT High Pass and Lowpass Filters

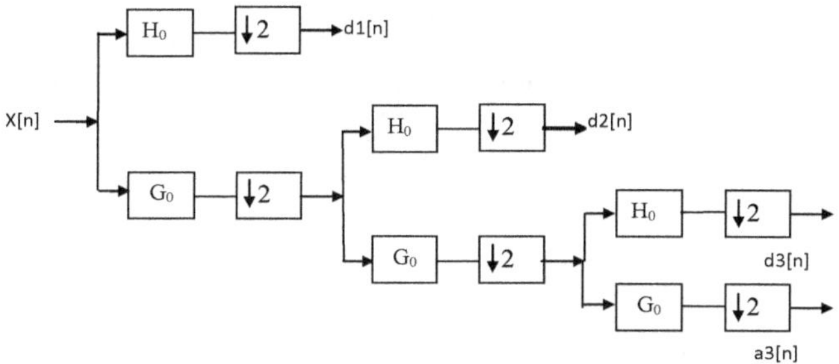

Figure 5.3: Three Level Wavelet Decomposition

5.3.3. Wavelet Packet Decomposition

The wavelet packet method is a generalization of wavelet decomposition that offers a richer range of possibilities for signal analysis and which allows the best matched analysis to a signal [Vimal Krishnan, 2009]. The WPD divides the low and also the high frequency subband of signal. In wavelet analysis, a signal is split into an approximation and a detail coefficient. The approximation coefficient is then itself split into a second-level approximation coefficients and detail coefficients, and the process is repeated. In wavelet packet analysis, the details as well as the approximations can be split. The top level of the WPD tree is the time representation of the signal. As each level of the tree is traversed there is an increase in the tradeoff between the time and frequency resolution. The bottom level of a fully decomposed tree is the frequency representation of the signal. Figure 5.4 shows the level 3 decomposition using wavelet packet transform.

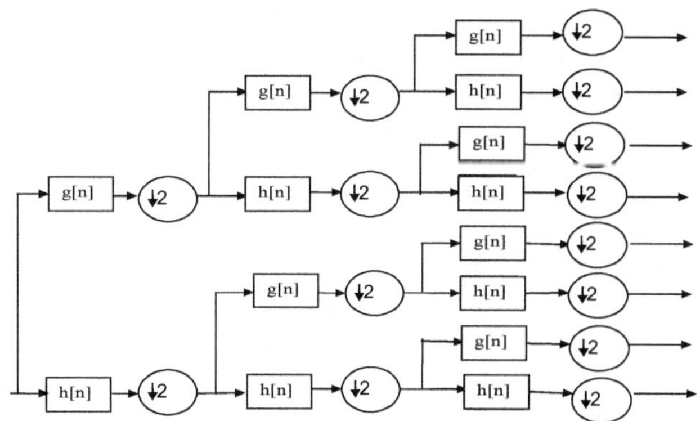

Figure 5.4: Three Level Wavelet Packet Decomposition Tree

The wavelet packet method is a generalization of wavelet decomposition that offers a richer signal analysis. Wavelet packet atoms are waveforms indexed by three naturally interpreted parameters: position and scale as in wavelet transform decomposition and frequency. In the following, the wavelet transform is defined as the inner product of a signal x(t) with the mother wavelet $\psi(t)$:

$$\psi_{a,b}(t) = \psi\left(\frac{t-b}{a}\right) \qquad (5.1)$$

$$\psi_{a,b}x(a,b) = \frac{1}{\sqrt{a}}\int_{-\infty}^{+\infty} x(t)\psi * z\left(\frac{t-b}{a}\right)dt \qquad (5.2)$$

where a and b are the scale and shift parameters, respectively. The mother wavelet may be dilated or translated by modulating a and b. The wavelet packets transform performs the recursive decomposition of the speech signal obtained by the recursive binary tree. Basically, the WPT is very similar to DWT but WPT decomposes both details and approximations instead of only performing the decomposition process on approximations. The principle of wavelet packet (WP) is that, given a signal, a pair of low-pass and high-pass filters is used to yield two sequences to capture different frequency sub-band features of the original signal.

5.4.   Haar Wavelet Transform

The Haar wavelet is the simplest type of wavelet. In discrete form, Haar wavelets are related to a mathematical operation called the Haar transform (HT). The Haar transform decomposes a discrete signal into two sub signals of half its length. While a signal has to be decomposed in terms of its constituent individual sinusoids (Fourier analysis) for spectral analysis and fast evaluation of the convolution operation, it is found that the decomposition of a signal in terms of its components corresponding to different bands of the frequency spectrum (wavelet transform analysis) is suitable for applications such as signal compression, with reduced computational complexity of $O(N)$ rather than $O(N \log_2 N)$. The discrete version of this transform, which is similar to the discrete Fourier transform (DFT), is called the discrete wavelet transform (DWT). The DWT can be interpreted as spectral analysis using a set of basic functions those are localized in both time and frequency, in contrast to the infinite-extent sinusoids used in Fourier analysis. The technical disadvantage of the Haar wavelet is that it is not continuous. This property can, however, be useful for the analysis of signals with sudden transitions. The basic Haar wavelet is a piecewise constant function that is defined as follows:

$$\psi_{[0,1]}(r) = \left\{ 1, 0 \leq r \leq \frac{1}{2} \; ; -1, 1 \leq r \leq \frac{1}{2} \; ; 0, \text{otherwise} \right.$$

The Haar transform decomposes a discrete signal into two sub signals of half its length. A HT decomposes each signal into two components, one is called average (approximation) and the other is known as difference.

5.5.   Daubechies Wavelet Transform

The Db4 wavelet transform, like the Haar transform, can be extended to multiple levels as many times as the signal length can be divided by 2. The extension is similar to the way the Haar transforms extended.

The Daubechies wavelet transforms are defined in the same way as the Haar wavelet transform by computing running aver-ages and differences via scalar products with scaling signals and wavelets the only difference between them consists in how these scaling signals and wavelets are defined. For the Daubechies wavelet transforms, the scaling signals and wavelets have slightly longer supports, i.e., they produce averages and differences using just a few more values from the signal. This slight change, however, provides a tremendous improvement in the capabilities of these new transforms. They provide us with a set of powerful tools for performing basic signal processing tasks. These tasks include compression and noise removal for audio signals and for images, and include image enhancement and signal recognition. There are many Daubechies transforms, but they are all very similar.

The Daubechies wavelets represent a collection of orthogonal mother wavelets with compact support, characterized by a maximal number of vanishing moments for some given length of the support. Corresponding to each mother wavelets from this class, there is a scaling function (also called father wavelet) which generates an orthogonal MRA. They provide us with a set of powerful tools for performing basic speech processing tasks. These tasks include compression and noise removal for audio signals and speech recognition. For example, a db4 wavelet and its scaling function are shown in figure 5.5.

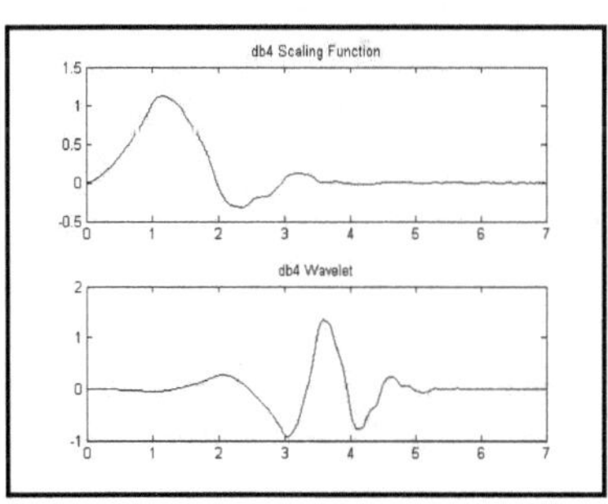

Figure 5.5: Plot of db4 Wavelet and its Scaling Function

The Daubechies wavelet transforms are defined in the same way as the Haar wavelet transform by computing the running averages and differences via scalar products with scaling signals and wavelets the only difference between them consists in how these scaling signals and wavelets are defined. The Daubechies wavelet is more complicated than the Haar wavelet. Daubechies wavelets are continuous; thus, they are more computationally expensive to use than the Haar wavelet.

5.6.   Symlet Wavelet Transform

Symlet (symN, where N is the order), also known as Daubechies least asymmetric mother wavelets. They are compact supported, orthogonal, continuous, but only nearly symmetric mother wavelets. The symlets are nearly symmetrical, orthogonal and biorthogonal wavelets proposed by Daubechies as modifications to the db family. The properties of the two wavelet families are similar. Here few wavelet are shown in figure 5.6. Symlets have the highest number of vanishing moments for a given support width. Symlets have N/2 vanishing moments, support length N-1 and filter length N. The properties of the two wavelet families are similar. There are 7 different Symlets functions from sym2 to sym8. The simlet scaling and wavelet function are shown in figure 5.6.

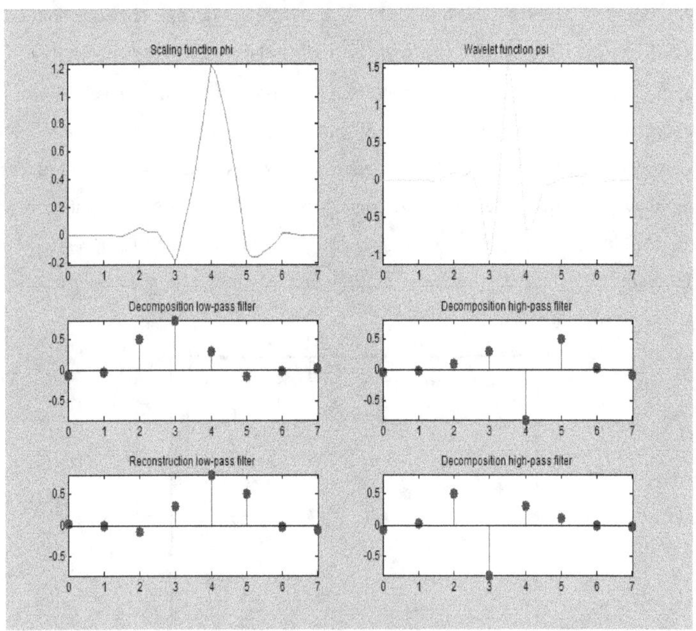

Figure 5.6: Simlet Wavelet

5.7. The Properties of Wavelets

The properties of wavelets which make they are useful tools for data mining and many other applications. A wavelet transformation converts data from an original domain to a wavelet domain by expanding the raw data in an orthonormal basis generated by dilation and translation of a father and mother wavelet. Wavelet transformation preserves the structure of data. The properties of wavelets are described as follows:

Computation Complexity

First, the computation of wavelet transform can be very efficient. Discrete Fourier transform requires $O(N^2)$ multiplications and fast Fourier transform also needs $O(N \log N)$ multiplications. However fast wavelet transform based on Mallat's pyramidal algorithm only needs $O(N)$ multiplications. The space complexity is also linear.

Vanishing Moments

Another important property of wavelets is vanishing moments. A function $f(x)$ which is supported in bounded region # is called to have n-vanishing moments if it satisfies the following equation:

$$\int_{\omega} f(x)x^j dx = 0, \quad j=0, 1,..., n. \qquad (5.3)$$

That is, the integrals of the product of the function and low degree polynomials are equal to zero. The intuition of vanishing moments of wavelets is the oscillatory nature which can be thought to be the characterization of difference or details between a data with the data in its neighborhood. Thus the vanishing moment property leads to many important wavelet techniques such as denoising and dimensionality reduction. The noisy data can usually be approximated by low-degree polynomial if the data are smooth in most of regions, therefore the corresponding wavelet coefficients are usually small which can be eliminated by setting a threshold.

Compact Support

Each wavelet basis function is supported on a finite interval. For example, the support of Haar function is [0,1]; the support of wavelet $db2$ is [0, 3]. Compact support guarantees the localization of wavelets. In other words, processing a region of data with wavelet does not affect the data out of this region.

Decorrelated Coefficients

Another important aspect of wavelets is their ability to reduce temporal correlation so that the correlation of wavelet coefficients is much smaller than the correlation of the corresponding temporal process.

Hence, the wavelet transform could be able used to reduce the complex process in the time domain into a much simpler process in the wavelet domain.

Parseval's Theorem

Assume that $e \in L^2$ and ψ_i be the orthonormal basis of L^2.

The Parseval's theorem states the following property of wavelet transform:

$$\| e \|_2^2 = \sum_i |< e_i \psi_i >|^2 \qquad (5.4)$$

In other words, the energy, which is defined to be the square of its L_2 norm, is preserved under the orthonormal wavelet transform. Hence the distances between any two objects are not changed by the transform.

5.8.   Wavelet Packet Decomposition and Sliding Frame based Model (WPDSFM) for Keyword Spotting

Isolated word recognition and speech similarity measurement has been a popular research topic. However, due to dynamic nature of continuous speech signal in terms of noise interference, time warping, connected speech and variability in frequency ranges; word identification becomes more challenging. To deal with the dynamics in speech signal, a combination of sliding frame window method with sequential processes is proposed in this system as shown. The WPDSFM keyword spotting algorithm is given in table 6.1 Time warped speech and background noise interference are the most challenging factors to deal with. The input speech is passed to pre-processing stage which enhances the speech quality in terms of silence removal, noise reduction, re-sampling and segmentation.

The wavelet packet decomposition is applied to the enhanced speech signal to acquire its frequency domain spectrum and filter out unwanted frequencies from input and template speech. The selected frequency spectrum is passed to feature extraction process that extracts some important features out of time and frequency domain speech signal. Finally, the Euclidean distance is calculated between test and template word's features that provides the similarity score.

5.8.1. WPDSFM KWS algorithm

Table 5.1: WPDSFM Keyword Spotting Algorithm

Given the features of the input signal S = {S_i : i=1,2,3,....n}where i is the frame index and **n** is the total number of frames in the input speech signal and the speech features of the keyword

K = {K_j: j = 1,2,3,.....m}

where j is the frame index and **m** is the total number of frames in the search keyword signal.

1. Consider a block of frames as X and l is the index of the speech block X and initially l is taken as 1.
2. From frames of input speech signal, m number of frames are selected from lth position as a block with the constraint l+m<= n.

$$Xl=\{Sa : a= l+1,.. l+m\}$$

3. Euclidean distance is used to calculate the similarity measure (dis) in between the features of keyword K and features of a block of input speech Xl .
4. The threshold value of similarity distance T is specified The similarity score **dis** is compared with the threshold value T.
5. If the **dis**<= T then Matching is found and the value of match count is incremented by 1
6. The value of l is added with m.
7. Else no matching is found
8. The value of l is added with 1.
9. The steps 2 to 5 are repeated until l+m exceeds n

5.8.2. Preprocessing

The test word and the template speech signal are passed to the pre-treatment component of the proposed system. Both signals are enhanced in terms of sampling, silence removal, windowing and background noise reduction. The sampling rate of 8 KHZ is given as user input for the implementation of the algorithm. After sample rate conversion, background noise is reduced to minimum level of signal to background noise ratio 2:1 based on the spectral subtraction performed in dependently in the frequency bands corresponding to the auditory critical bands. The short time energy measurement of a speech signal can be used to determine voiced/unvoiced speech. The energy of voiced speech is much greater than the energy of unvoiced speech. The energy and the zero crossing rates features are used for silence removal of the speech.

5.8.3. Framing and WPD Transformation

The properties of speech waveform can be assumed to remain relatively constant due to slow varying nature of speech signal over a short period of time called frame. Framing is a process of decomposing the speech signal into smaller units. After silence removal, the speech signal is reconstructed by combining all the selected frames. The research experiments are conducted on frame by frame analysis of template speech signal. Each frame has an equal size of test word and is composed of a number of small *blocks* with 20-30 *msec* duration. The test frame is progressed along the template speech. At each time step, the similarity score is calculated and stored along with the template frame position in a vector. At the end of template speech signal, a threshold (0.6) value is applied to the calculated similarity score vector and the corresponding locations of best matched words are retrieved.

In the proposed system, the wavelet packet decomposition is applied to the enhanced speech signal to acquire its frequency domain spectrum and filter out unwanted frequencies from input and template speech. Extracted features provide better results when they do not loose class related information. The wavelets are powerful general-purpose tools for speech signal processing and spectral analysis. Using Wavelets Packets, speech signal can be represented by integral of different forms of mother wavelet that are produced by scaling and shifting process. Haar, Daubhecies and Symlet wavelet packet decompositions have been successfully used as a spectral analysis tool.

5.8.4. *Extraction of WPD based Statistical Features*

Feature extraction is the process of finding out dominant features out of time and frequency domain signal that might contain enough acoustic information for a word to be identified.

The selected frequency spectrum is passed to feature extraction process that extracts some important features out of time and frequency domain speech signal. Below are the features that are used for the test and template frame matching.

- RMS (Root Mean Square level)
- Correlation
- Homogeneity
- Standard Deviation
- Variance
- Smoothness
- Kurtosis
- Skewness

The extracted features for both test and template frames are passed to Euclidean distance to measure the similarity score.

5.9.   Functionality of the Algorithm

The method uses wavelet packet decomposition and sliding frame window method to implement the keyword spotting. The sliding frame window blocks the speech into a block of frames such that the number of frames in the block is equal to number of frames of the keyword signal are selected from the input signal starting from the first frame. This block of feature vectors is used for finding similarity measure using Euclidean distance. If the word corresponding to the block of frames is same as the keyword then the score is the minimum. If the word corresponding to the block of frames is completely different from the keyword, the feature vectors from the block may not fall into the distribution and the similarity measure gives high score. Likewise, the next possibility is the word corresponding to the block of frames is partially similar to the keyword. If this is the case, the similarity score of the block will be in between the above two values. If the obtained score is within the limit of the specified threshold, then the matching count is incremented by one. After the above processing of the current block, the block is shifted by one frame to the right. Then the entire procedure is repeated for this new block and the similarity score is obtained. Likewise the scores are obtained andmatching is counted until the tail end of the block reaches the last frame of the speech frames.

The performance of the proposed keyword spotting algorithm is assessed in terms of detection rate which is defined as

$$\text{Detection Rate} = \frac{n_c}{n_c + n_i + n_r} \qquad (5.5)$$

Where n_c = Number of correctly classified keywords; n_i=Number of incorrectly classified keywords; n_r = Number of rejected keywords.

CHAPTER 6

WAVELET–NEURAL NETWORK BASED KEYWORD SPOTTING

6.1.   Introduction

Neural Networks (NN) are important data mining tool used for classification and clustering. It is an attempt to build machine that will mimic brain activities and be able to learn. NN usually learns by examples. If NN is supplied with enough examples, it should be able to perform classification and even discover new trends or patterns in data. Basic NN is composed of three layers, input, output and hidden layer.

Each layer can have number of nodes and nodes from input layer are connected to the nodes from hidden layer. Nodes from hidden layer are connected to the nodes from output layer. Those connections represent weights between nodes. There are two types of NN based on learning technique, they can be supervised where output values are known beforehand (back propagation algorithm) and unsupervised where output values are not known (clustering).

Classification is grouping of the objects or things that are similar. Examples of classifications are found everywhere, supermarkets put similar things together, there are shelf for meat, diary products, cleaning products. Classifications makes life easier, like in supermarket example, if things were put on shelf in random order, it would make shopping unpleasant and lengthy experience. Most financial institutions use classification for their credit ratings, medicine uses it extensively for diagnosing diseases. There are many classification techniques used in data mining with NN being one of them.

NN model is explained in this paper but distinction has to be made between NN in humans and animals and NN that are being used in industries. Former NN are often called Artificial NN and they will be discussed in paper but for simplicity they will be referred to as NN.

There are two types of NN based on learning technique, they can be supervised where output values are known beforehand (back propagation algorithm) and unsupervised where output values are not known (clustering).

NN architecture, number of nodes to choose, how to set the weights between the nodes, training the network and evaluating the results are covered. Activation function gets mentioned together with learning rate, momentum and pruning. Back propagation algorithm, probably the most popular NN algorithm is demonstrated.

6.2. Wavelets and Neural Network

Neural networks are developed to emulate the human brain that is powerful, flexible and efficient. However, conventional networks only process the signal on its finest resolution. It is however not the case for human brain. For example, the retinal image is likely to be processed in separate frequency channels. The introduction of wavelet decomposition provides a new tool for approximation. Inspired by both the MLP and wavelet decomposition, a wavelet network is developed. This has caused rapid development of a new bred of neural network model integrated with wavelets. Most researchers used wavelets as radial basis functions that allow hierarchical, multi-resolution learning of input-output maps from experimental data. The wavelets are used to break the signal down into its multi-resolution components before feeding them into a MLP. We show that the wavelet MLP neural network is capable of utilizing the time-frequency information to improve its consistency in performance.

Wavelet theory provides a unified framework for a number of techniques that had been developed independently for various signals processing application, e.g., multiresolution signal processing used in computer vision; subband coding, developed for speech and image compression; and wavelet series expansions, developed in applied mathematics. In this section, we will concentrate on the multiresolution approximation that is utilized in the presented model.

6.3. Back Propagation (BP) Algorithm

One of the most popular NN algorithms is back propagation algorithm. Conceptually, a network forward propagates activation to produce an output and it backward propagates error to determine weight changes. The weights on the connections between neurons mediate the passed values in both directions. The Back propagation algorithm is used to learn the weights of a multilayer neural network with a fixed architecture. It performs gradient descent to try to minimize the sum squared error between the network's output values and the given target values. Rojas [2005] claimed that BP algorithm could be broken down to four main steps. After choosing the weights of the network randomly, the back propagation algorithm is used to compute the necessary corrections. The algorithm can be decomposed in the following four steps:

Table 6.1: Back Propagation Algorithm

1.Feed-forward computation
2. Back propagation to the output layer
3. Back propagation to the hidden layer
4. Weight updates

The algorithm is stopped when the value of the error function has become sufficiently small. This is very rough and basic formula for BP algorithm.

There are some variation proposed by other scientist but Rojas definition seem to be quite accurate and easy to follow. The last step, weight updates is happening throughout the algorithm.

6.3.1. *Feed-forward Computation*

Feed forward computation or forward pass is two-step process. First part is getting the values of the hidden layer nodes and second part is using those values from hidden layer to compute value or values of output layer.

6.3.2. *Back Propagation to the Output Layer*

Once error is known, it will be used for backward propagation and weights adjustment.

It is two-step process. Error is propagated from output layer to the hidden layer first. This is where learning rate and momentum are brought to equation.

6.3.3. *Back Propagation to the Hidden Layer*

Errors have to be propagated from hidden layer down to the input layer. This is bit more complicated than propagating error from output to hidden layer.

6.4. Wavelet Packet and Neural Network Model (WPDNNM) based Keyword Spotting Design

The backward propagation of errors or back propagation, is a common method of training artificial neural networks and used in conjunction with an optimization method such as gradient descent.

The algorithm repeats a two phase cycle, propagation and weight update. When an input vector is presented to the network, it is propagated forward through the network, layer by layer, until it reaches the output layer. The output of the network is then compared to the desired output, using a loss function, and an error value is calculated for each of the neurons in the output layer.

The error values are then propagated backwards, starting from the output, until each neuron has an associated error value which roughly represents its contribution to the original output.

6.4.1. *Wavelet Packet and Neural Network Model (WPDNNM) Keyword Spotting Algorithm*

Table 6.2: The WPDNNM Keyword Spotting Algorithm

Inputting Signal and keyword

Step 1: Input the speech signal

Step 2 : Input the keywords to train

Step 3 : Set the variables

Step 4: Select Wavelet Packet

Preprocessing

Preprocessing is done with moving average filter

Step 5: Preprocess and Frame the signal

Wavelet Packet Decomposition based Feature Extraction

Step 6:The WPD based statistical features RMS, Energy, Standard Deviation, Variance and Skewness are calculated.

Network Training

Step 7: Initialize weights

Step 8: While stopping condition is false, do steps 2 to 9

Step 9: For each training pair, do steps 3 - 8

Feed forward

Step 10: Input unit receives input signal and propagates it to all units in the hidden layer

Step 11: Each hidden unit sums its weighted input signals

Step 12:Each output unit sums its weighted input signals and applied its activation function to compute its output signal.

Back Propagation Neural Network Training

Step 13: Each output unit receives a target pattern corresponding to the input training pattern, computes its error information to units in the layer below

Step 14: Each hidden unit sums its delta inputs

Testing Keyword

Step 15:Simualtion value is calculated using simulation function and set a threshold value

Keyword Identification

Step 16: Identify the occurrences of keyword if its value is less than the threshold

Repeat the step 15 and 16 for the entire speech frames.

The algorithm WPDNNM is explained in a block diagram as shown in Figure 6.1

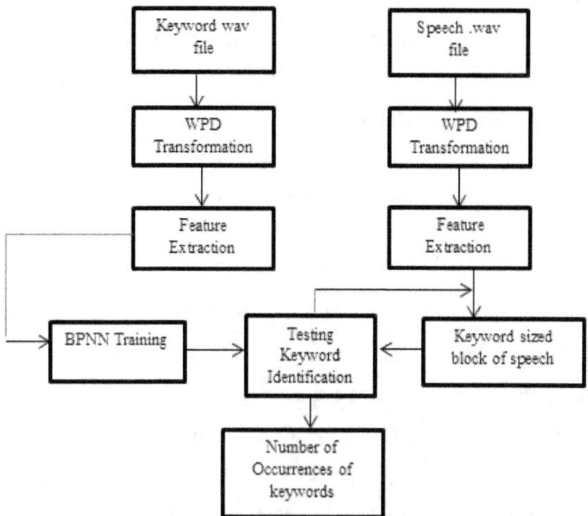

Figure 6.1: Block Diagram of Wavelet-neural (WPDNNM) Keyword Spotting Approach

6.4.2. *Speech Preprocessing*

Speech signal pre-processing covers digital filtering, to enhance the speech quality in terms of silence removal, noise reduction, resampling and segmentation. In this system moving–average filter function is used to filter the input speech and keyword given. The moving average filter is a simple Low Pass FIR (Finite Impulse Response)

6.4.3. *Multi-wavelet Packet Transformation*

The decomposed frequency spectrum is passed to feature extraction process that extracts some important features out of time and frequency domain speech signal. The features which are extracted and used for the test and template frame matching are discussed in the previous chapter.

6.4.4. *Network Training*

The performance of the system depends on the neural network model deployed to identify the words in the input data. Back Propagation algorithm which is based on the concept of improving the network performance by reduction of error from the output data is used to train the network in this system. This algorithm works in batch mode in which the weight updates take place after much propagation. The implementation of this algorithm is faster and efficient depending upon the amount of input-output data available in the layers.

Before training the feed forward network, the weight and biases are initialized. Once the network weights and biases have been initialized, the network is ready for training. We used random numbers around zero to initialize weights and biases in the network. The training process requires a set of proper inputs and targets as outputs. During training, the weights and biases of the network are iteratively adjusted to minimize the network performance function. The default performance function for feed forward networks is mean square errors, the average squared errors between the network outputs and the target output.

6.5. Functionality of the Algorithm

In the wavelet–neural approach, Wavelet packet decomposition based features are used with back propagation neural network classifier. Speech file of 5 minutes length is used in this experiment. Three spoken keywords are used in the experiment for training the network. Recording is done in a silent room. The speech content and keywords are decomposed with Haar, Daubechies 2 and Simlet 4 wavelet packets. The input speech files and keywords are the same which are represented in the previous chapter in tanel 6.2 and 6.3 respectively.

The system for keyword spotting using the NWPM algorithm is implemented in MATLABR (2014a). Testing is done with the selected speech file and the selected keywords. The processing steps are discussed below.

1. *Loading a Signal*

Loading a speech signal. For example d_one.wav is loaded as keyword and wav1_file is taken as input speech file. Set the sampling rate R = 8000Hz

2. *Preprocessing of the Signal is Done*

    select the wavelet type 1 or 2 or 3 for the variable w

    Number 1 is selected for "Haar".

    Number 2 is selected for "Db2".

    Number 3 is selected for "Simlets".

    Value 2 is selected for wavelet Db2.

3. *Performing Wavelet Decomposition of a Signal*

    To perform a level 3 decomposition of the signal, execute the command

    [C,L]=wpdec (X, 3,'db2') which returns a wavelet packet tree corresponding to the wavelet packet decomposition of the vector X at level 3, with the wavelet db2 wavelet. The coefficients of all the components of a third-level decomposition (that is, the third-level approximation and the first three levels of detail) are returned concatenated into one vector, C. Vector L gives the lengths of each component.

4. *Extracting Approximation and Detail Coefficients*

To extract the level 3 approximation and detail coefficients from C, the command is wpcoef implemented. It is a one or two-dimensional wavelet packet analysis function.

X = wpcoef(C,N) returns the coefficients associated with the node N of the wavelet packet tree C. The approximation and details coefficients of Db2wavelet is shown in figure 6.2.

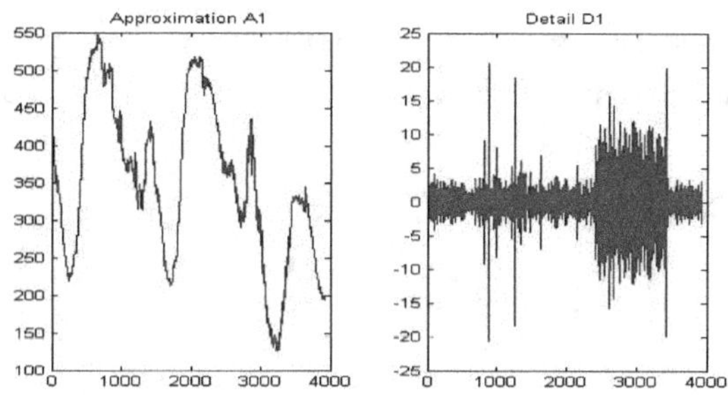

Figure 6.2: The Approximation and Details Coefficients of Db2 Wavelet

5. *Statistical Feature Extraction*

Various statistical feature extraction are extracted using various matlab functions as follows:

```
glcms = graycomatrix(X)
stats = graycoprops(glcms)
RMS = rms(X)
Correlation = corr(X)
Energy = ene(X)
Homogeneity – stats.Homogeneity
Standard_Deviation = std(X)
Variance = mean (X)
a = sum(double(X)
Smoothness = 1-(1/(1+a))
Kurtosis = kurtosis(double(X)
Skewness = skewness(double(X)
```

6. *BPNN Classifier*

BPNN is trained with the feature of the keywords using train.m function with the following input and output parameters. Train.m trains a network net according to net.trainFcn and net.trainParam. Typically one epoch of training is defined as a single presentation of all input vectors to the network. The network is then updated according to the results of all those presentations. Training occurs until a maximum number of epochs occurs, the performance goal is met, or any other stopping condition of the function net.trainFcn occurs.

7. *Testing with BPNN Classifier*

After training the network, the network is trained with a test set, using the sim().m function by giving the trained network and the test samples as input arguments.

CHAPTER 7

MULTIWAVELET PACKET ENTROPY MODEL BASED KEYWORD SPOTTING

7.1. Introduction

Multiwavelet packets possess better properties than traditional wavelets. Multiwavelet packet transformation has more high-frequency information. Spectral entropy can be applied as an analysis index to the complexity or uncertainty of a signal. Multiwavelet packet energy entropy, time entropy, Shannon singular entropy, and Tsallis singular entropy are defined as the feature extraction methods of signals.

A natural approach to quantify the degree of order of a complex signal is to consider its spectral entropy, as defined from the Fourier power spectrum (Powell and Percival, 1979). The spectral entropy is a measure of how concentrated or widespread the Fourier power spectrum of a signal is. An ordered activity, like a sinusoidal signal, is manifested as a narrow peak in the frequency domain. This concentration of the frequency spectrum in one single peak corresponds to a low entropy value. On the other extreme, a disordered activity will have a wide band response in the frequency domain, thus being reflected in higher entropies. The disadvantages of the spectral entropy defined from the FT can be partially resolved by using a short time Fourier transform (STFT). Powell and Percival [1979] defined a time evolving entropy from STFT by using a Hanning window. With this approach, FT is applied to time-evolving windows of a few seconds of data refined with an appropriate function. Then, the evolution of the frequencies can be followed and the stationary requirement is partially satisfied by considering the signals as quasi-stationary for a few seconds. Due to the uncertainty principle, one critical limitation appears when windowing data, if the window is too narrow, the frequency resolution will be poor; and if the window is too wide, the time localization will be less precise. To overcome these limitations a time evolving entropy can be defined from a time–frequency representation of the signal as provided by the wavelet transform [Blanco et al., 1998; Quian Quiroga et al., 2000].

In this model, four entropies with the multiwavelet packet to extract the features of speech signal are proposed. These features are used as training samples of the Back Propagation neural network, which are trained to implement transient signal classification and keyword identification. Multiwavelets packets can simultaneously possess orthogonality, symmetry, short support, and high-order vanish moments. In addition, there is more low and high-frequency information of multiwavelet decomposition than with conventional wavelets. The multiwavelet packet approach is an extension of multiwavelets. It offers more high-frequency information than multiwavelets. Wavelet transform is commonly used to extract characteristic quantities, while BPNN is used classify characteristic quantities. Spectral entropy based on Shannon entropy is a tool for producing an index of the complexity or uncertainty of a signal or system. Wavelet transformation is capable of revealing features of data that other signal analysis techniques may miss, and satisfies the need to analyze transient signals. A combination of wavelet transformation and entropy is proposed and applied to a number of applications.

7.2.   Moving Wavelet Packet to Multiwavelet Packet

When wavelet transform is used to decompose the signals, the high-frequency resolution of signals is very low. Wavelet packet is a generalization of wavelet bases by taking linear combinations of the traditional wavelet functions to form a function cluster. Wavelet packet transform can provide more detailed decomposition of high frequency components. These decompositions are redundant and have no omissions. The results of wavelet packet transform can represent the complexity of signals more accurately and can obtain better time-frequency analysis.

Wavelet transform is a powerful tool to detect both stationary and transient signals. The wavelet transform technique has special benefits for describing signals at various localization levels in time, in addition to frequency domains [Wu and Chen, J.C, 2006], [Bafroui, 2014]. Discrete wavelet transform is obtained by discretizing the scaling and shifting parameters in continuous wavelet transform.

The discrete wavelet transform can be efficiently realized by means of a pair of low-pass and high-pass wavelet filters. Through such a pair of filters, the signal is decomposed into low and high-frequency components, respectively. The approximation coefficient represents the low-frequency component of the signal, and the detail coefficient corresponds to the high-frequency component. Usually, through the Mallat algorithm, a signal is decomposed and reconstructed in multi-scale.

7.3.   Multiwavelets and Multiwavelet Packets

7.3.1.   Multiwavelet Transformation

Multiwavelets concept is introduced with properties of scaling functions and wavelet functions. Symmetric scaling functions constructed by Geronimo *et al.* [Geronimo, 1996] had short support, generated an orthogonal multiresolution analysis (MRA), and provided approximation order two, for wavelets known as GHM multiwavelets.

Chui and Lian [1996] constructed two multiplicity multiscaling functions and multiwavelet functions with symmetry through the study of orthogonality, tight support, symmetry, and interpolation of multiwavelets. In wavelet analysis, the MRA is produced based on a scaling function and the base of space $L^2(R)$ constructed by the translation and dilation of wavelet function. The MRA is critical in conventional wavelets transformation. Similarly, the multiresolution in multiwavelets analysis also takes place in multiwavelet analysis. However, the MRA is produced through several scaling functions and the base of space $L^2(R)$ constructed by the translation and dilation of multiwavelet functions. These multiwavelet functions are called multiwavelets.

7.3.2. *Multiwavelet Packet Transformation*

Multiwavelet packet transformation is an extension of multiwavelet transformation. Consider S0 be the original signal. For wavelet packet decomposition, let L1 and H1 be the low and highfrequency parts of wavelet transformation at scale 1. Let LL2 and LH2 be the low- and high-frequency parts of L1 decomposition, HL2 and HH2 be the low and high-frequency parts of H1 decomposition at scale 2. Let LLL3 and LLH3 be the low and high-frequency parts of LL2 decomposition, LHL3 and LHH3 be the low and high frequency parts of LH2 decomposition, HLL3 and HLH3 be the low and high-frequency parts of HL2 decomposition, and HHL3 and HHH3 be the low and high-frequency parts of HH2 decomposition at scale 3. The frame of the multiwavelet packet decomposition is shown in Figure 7.1, where the multiplicity is two. Because multiwavelet packet transformation is used to obtain more transient information in this paper, discuss the problem of the best multiwavelet packet. The choice of best multiwavelet packet may be found in [Z. G. Liu et al 2005].

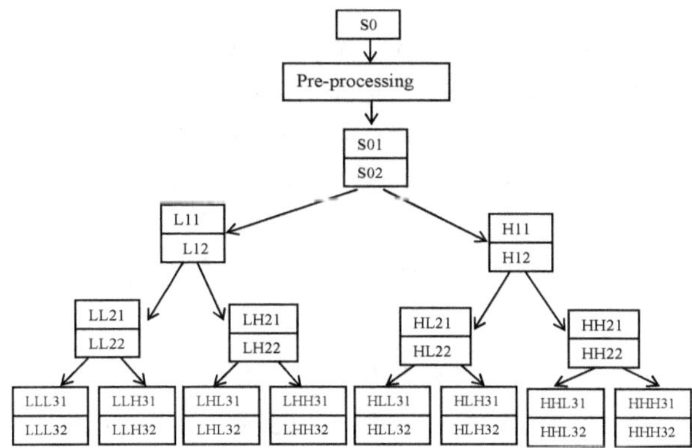

Figure 7.1: Frame of Multiwavelet e-packet Decomposition

7.4. Entropy and Multiwavelet Packet

Entropy is a kind of measurement of disorders, such as unsystematic, unbalance, and uncertainty. The uncertainty of any event is associated with its states and probabilities. The information entropy of X can be defined in [Shannon, 1948]

$$H(X) = -\sum_{j=1}^{L} p_{j\log(p_j)}$$

Where $p_j = 0$, $p\,j\log_{(p\,j)} = 0$.

7.4.1. Shannon Entropy

Shannon entropy is built based on Boltzmann–Gibbs (BG)entropy in thermo dynamics, which is extensive [C. Tsallis, 1988]. Hence, Shannon entropy is extensive as well. Some experiments show that the decomposition or reconstruction coefficients of some signals are non extensive [J. K. Chen, 2010]. The extensive property means that if the system is composed of two independent subsystems A and B, the entropy H $(A+B)$ of system satisfies the additive property

$$H(A + B)/k = H(A)/k + H(B)/k$$

Where k is the Boltzmann constant. Based on the above equation, the signal's entropy should be the sum of entropy in each scale through the decomposition and reconstruction of the signal with multiwavelet packet. Because frequency aliasing and energy leakage are found in the multiwavelet packet, the equation is not satisfied. Hence, Tsallis entropy, which is non-extensive, is introduced in this paper. Tsallis entropy can provide the correct physical expression for non- additive systems with mixtures or irregular fragments.

Shannon entropy and Tsallis entropy may be considered as the system's information measurement under some state, and can be adopted to estimate the complexity of random signals. The transient fault signals of transmission line contain a great deal of transient, random, and uncertain information. For the transient protection in power systems, it is difficult not only to distinguish faults inside or outside the protection zone but also to distinguish fault transients from transients of normal operations. Hence, comprehensive fault transient information for fault recognition and classification is crucial.

7.4.2. Multiwavelet Packet Energy Entropy

Let $E = E_1, E_2, \ldots, E_k, \ldots, E_2{}^{J+1}$ be the multiwavelet packet energy spectrum of $x(t)$ on the j th scale, E can be considered as a signal energy division on the scale domain, where J is the level number of multiwavelet packet decomposition, $j \in N$, and $k \in [1, 2^{J+1}]$.

According to the orthogonality of multiwavelet transformation, in some time window (window width $w \in N$), the total E of the signal is equal to the sum of all components E_k.

$$\text{Let } P_k = E_k/E, \text{ then } \sum_1^{2^{j+1}} P_k = 1$$

The multiwavelet packet energy entropyis defined as

$$W_{EE} = \sum_k P_k \log P_k$$

With the moving window, the variation law of multiwavelet packet entropy with respect to the time can be obtained. The corresponding relationship between the scale domain and frequency domain can be described.

7.4.3. *Multiwavelet Packet Time Entropy*

If a moving window ($w \in N$) for the results of multiwavelet packet transformation is defined, the moving window can be described by $w(m; w, \delta) = \{d_j(k), k = 1 + m\delta, \ldots, w + m\delta\}$,where δ represents the moving factor of the defined window and $\delta \in N$, $m = 1, 2, \ldots, M, M \in N$. The moving window can be divided into L, $L \in N$ spaces $w(misfies, s0 = \min[W(m; w, \delta)]$, and $s_L = \max[W(m; w, \delta)]$.

Definition 2: Suppose $P^m(Zl)$represent the possibility of multiwavelet packet coefficients $d_{j,r}$ $(k) \in W(m; w, \delta)$, $r = 2$ in the section Zl, namely the ratio of the number in the section Zl and $w(m; w, \delta)$. The multiwavelet packet time entropy can be defined as

$$E_{TEj} = -\sum P^m(Z_l) \log(P^m(Z_l))$$

7.4.4. *MultiwaveletTsallis Singular Entropy*

The decomposition results of multiwavelet packet can be used to construct a m×n matrix $Dm×n$. Based on the singular value decomposition theory, for a $m \times n$ matrix D, there must be a $m \times l$ matrix U, a $l \times n$ matrix V, and a $l \times l$ matrix $\wedge$ .The matrix D can be decomposed by $Dm×n = U_{m×l} \wedge_{l×l} V_{l×n}$. The diagonal elements λ_i $(i = 1, 2, \ldots, l)$ of diagonal matrix $\wedge$ are nonnegative and arranged in descending order. $\lambda_1 \geq \lambda_2 \geq \cdots \geq \lambda_l \geq 0$.

The diagonal elements are the singular values of the decomposition results matrix $Dm×n$ of the multiwavelet packet. When there is no noise or high signal to noise in the signal, most of the main diagonal singular values are zero. In addition, if the signal has fewer frequency components, the decomposition results of the multiwavelet packet have fewer nonzero singular values.

7.5.   Back Propagation Neural Network

Input vectors and corresponding target vectors are used to train a network until it can approximate a function, associate input vectors with specific output vectors, or classify input vectors in an appropriate way as defined in this study. The network consists of three layers: input layer, output layer and the intermediate layer i.e. the hidden layer. These layers comprises of the neurons which are connected to form the entire network. Weights are assigned on the connections which marks the signal strength. The weight values are computed based on the input signal and the error function back propagated to the input layer. Networks with biases, a sigmoid layer and a linear output layer are capable of approximating any function with a finite number of discontinuities. The back propagation algorithm consists of two paths; forward path and backward path. Forward path contain creating a feed forward network, initializing weight, simulation and training the network. The network weights and biases are updated in backward path. The neural network model is shown in figure 7.2.

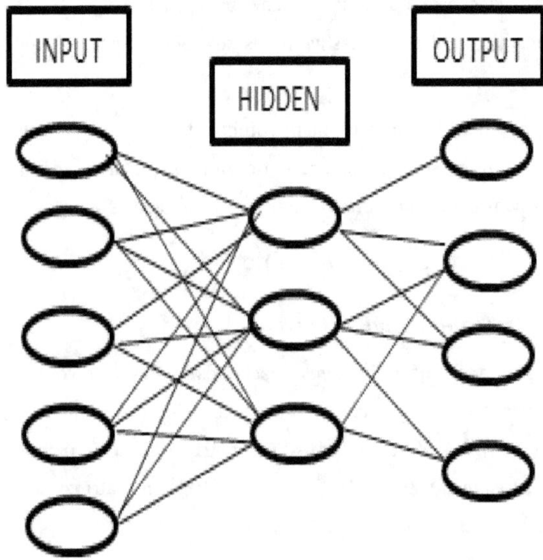

Figure 7.2: The Neural Network Model

7.6.   Multiwavelet Packet Entropy Model for Keyword Spotting

An algorithm Multiwavelet Packet Entropy Model (MWPEM) is used for keyword spotting using multiwavelet packet entropies.

7.6.1. *The MWPEM KWS Algorithm*

Table 7.1: The MWPEM Keyword Spotting Algorithm

Inputting Signal and keyword

Step 1: Input the speech signal

Step 2 : Input the keywords to train

Step 3 : Set the variables

Step 4: Select MultiWaveletPacket and Entropy

Preprocessing

Preprocessing is done with moving average filter

Step 5: Preprocess and Frame the signal

Multiwavelet Packet Entropy based Feature Extraction

Step 6: The Multiwavelet Packet Entropy is calculated using **wentropy** function

Network Training

Step 7: Initialize weights

 Step 8: While stopping condition is false, do steps 2 to 9

Step 9: For each training pair, do steps 3 - 8

Feed forward

Step 10: Input unit receives input signal and propagates it to all units in the hidden layer

Step 11: Each hidden unit sums its weighted input signals

Step 12: Each output unit sums its weighted input signals and applied its activation function to compute its output signal.

Back Propagation Neural Network Training

Step 13: Each output unit receives a target pattern corresponding to the input training pattern, computes its error information to units in the layer below

Step 14: Each hidden unit sums its delta inputs

Testing Keyword

Step 15:Simualtion value is calculated using simulation function and set a threshold value

Keyword Identification

Step 16: Identify the occurrences of keyword if its value is less than the threshold

Repeat the step 15 and 16 for the entire speech frames.

7.6.2. *Decomposition of Speech with Wavelet Packet and Multiwavelet Packet*

For the equality of comparison,DB4 wavelet packet is adopted for the decomposition of fault signals. Its filter length is equal to that of GHM, CL3, and SA4 multiwavelet packets. These multiwavelets are commonly used. The decomposition level number of waveletpacket and multiwavelet packet is three. As the choice reference of preprocessing and post processing methods in general, we use the GHM in it. Preprocessing method for the GHM multiwavelet, the balance preprocessing method for SA4and CL3 multiwavelets.

7.6.3. *Calculation of Entropies*

The multiwavelet packet entropies defined in the paper, including multiwavelet packet energy entropy, time entropy, Shannon singular entropy, and Tsallis singular entropy, are used to calculate the entropy values for the decomposition results of fault currents with wavelet and multiwavelet packets

7.6.4. *Training with BPNN Classifier*

After the calculation of the entropy values for the decomposition results of keyword of the input with wavelet packet and multiwavelet packet, the results are input into an BP neural network as the training eigen vectors. Through the training of the RBF neural network, the type of speech can be recognized and classified based on the different input signals. The input and output dimensions of the network are denoted by L and T, respectively, while M is the number of hidden nodes.

7.7. Functionality of Algorithm

Multiwavelet packet entropy based keyword spotting algorithm MWPEM is designed with BP neural network. To test the WPDSFM model, ten speech files with varying length are recorded. Five female and five male voices are recorded with the set of speech content. Ten speech files of length in range 30 sec to 1 min. are recorded in a noisy environment. Multiwavelet packet energy entropy, time entropy, Shannon singular entropy, and Tsallis singular entropy are defined as the features for designing KWS system. These features are used as training samples of the Back Propagation neural network, which are trained to implement transient signal classification and keyword identification.

Multiwavelets packets can simultaneously possess orthogonality, symmetry, short support, and high-order vanish moments.In addition, there is more low and high-frequency information of multiwavelet decomposition than with conventional wavelets. It offers more high-frequency information than multiwavelets. Spectral entropy based on Shannon entropy is used as a tool for producing an index of the complexity or uncertainty of a signal. Multiwaveletpacket is capable of revealing features of data that other signal analysis techniques may miss, and satisfies the need to analyze transient signals.

A combination of multiwavelet packet transformation and entropy is used and evaluated as a novel method for keyword spotting. The system for keyword spotting using the MWPEM algorithm is implemented in MATLAB R (2014a). Testing is done with given set of input speech and keywords. Step by step testing details are given below:

Testing the Model

1. *Loading a Signal*

   The wave file d_one.wav is loaded. Set the sampling rate R = 8000Hz

2. *Preprocessing of the Signal*

   Preprocessing is done with moving average filter. Speech signal pre-processing covers digital filtering, to enhance the speech quality in terms of silence removal, noise reduction, resampling and segmentation.

   In this proposed system moving–average filter function is used to filter the input speech and keyword given. The moving average filter is a simple Low Pass FIR(Finite Impulse Response) filter commonly used for smoothing signals. The moving average filter takes average of samples for filtering the noise from signal. The preprocessed output is then passed to the next stage multiwavelet packet decomposition. X is the preprocessed and sampled input signal

3. *Select the Entropy Type*

   Number 1 is selected for "Shannon".

   Number 2 is selected for "Energy".

   Number 3 is selected for "Time".

   Number 3 is selected for "Tsallis".

4. *Select the wavelet type 1 or 2 or 3 for the variable w*

   Number 1 is selected for "Haar".

   Number 2 is selected for "Db2".

   Number 3 is selected for "Simlets".

5. *Performing a Multilevel Wavelet Decomposition of a Signal.*

To perform a level 3 decomposition of the signal, execute the command

[C,L]=wpdec (X, 3,'db2')which returns a wavelet packet tree corresponding to the wavelet packet decomposition of the vector X at level 3, with the wavelet db2 wavelet. The coefficients of all the components of a third-level decomposition (that is, the third-level approximation and the first three levels of detail) are returned concatenated into one vector, C. Vector L gives the lengths of each component.

6. *Extracting Approximation and Detail Coefficients*

To extract the level 3 approximation and detail coefficients from C, the command is wpcoef implemented. It is a one or two-dimensional wavelet packet analysis function.

X = wpcoef(C,N) returns the coefficients associated with the node N of the wavelet packet tree C.

Computing Multiwavelet Packet Entropies

7. *BPNN Classifier Training*

BPNN is trained with the feature of the keywords using train() function with the following input and output parameters.

8. *Testing with BPNN Classifier*

Set the threshold value.

Testing is done with *sim*.m function. Compare the simulation value with the given threshold.

The result obtained from the algorithm with various entropies are compared. The performance of the proposed keyword spotting algorithm is assessed in terms of detection rate which is defined as

$$\text{Detection Rate} = \frac{n_c}{n_c + n_i + n_r}$$

Where n_c= Number of correctly classified keywords; n_i=Number of incorrectly classified keywords; n_r = Number of rejected keywords.